PLAIN
SAILING

PLAIN SAILING
LEARNING TO SEE LIKE A SAILOR

A SAIL TRIM MANUAL

DALLAS MURPHY

BURFORD BOOKS

Illustrations by Melanie Roher unless otherwise credited.
Book design by Melanie Roher.

Printed in the United States of America.

10   9   8   7   6   5   4   3   2   1

Library of Congress Cataloging-in-Publication Data is on file with the Library of Congress.

CONTENTS

8 | Tides and Current Sailing 145

9 | Safety 153

In Conclusion | 159

ACKNOWLEDGMENTS

All my thanks to the following people for their various valuable contributions to this book: Peter Burford, Betsy Frawley Haggerty, John Kretschmer, Nick Lansing, Paul Mirto, Melanie Roher, John Rousmaniere, Michael Rubin, Jonathan Russo, Steve Schwartz, John Toole, and Lydia Wills.

FOREWORD

Dallas Murphy's *Plain Sailing* is something of a marvel. While there are plenty of books about every aspect of sailing, a pursuit that's documented almost to excess, *Plain Sailing* manages to stand out. Few if any books especially those aimed at new sailors concentrate on sailing's essential element—wind.

Murphy, a writer by profession and a sailor by passion, shows you how to see like a sailor. And this is no small accomplishment. After reading his book, I thought, 'of course, this is how you learn to sail.' It seemed simple, obvious, logical, intuitive, this focus on wind, and I realized that by accident and good luck I had learned to sail Murphy's way.

All sailing manuals offer diagrams of triangles and vectors with shooting arrows and confusing vernacular that give new sailors pause. Murphy concedes that you will have to commit certain terms to memory, but that's more about being comfortable around other sailors than about learning to sail. You will need to know the names of certain sailboat parts; you will need to know what line corresponds to what action, but drilling them into your brain's hard drive does little to help you understand why you should ease the mainsheet and tighten the boom vang when running before the wind.

Plain Sailing is refreshing; reading it is like feeling the breeze on your cheeks. Sailing is, after all, all about wind. Only a non-sailor would think wind is invisible—when you finish *Plain Sailing* you'll understand. Seeing like a sailor is more important than thinking like a sailor.

I've done some serious sailing with Dallas Murphy, and I can attest that the man is not only a fine shipmate, he's a terrific sailor. He strikes me as a natural, but he swears he had to learn the ways of the wind. One thing is certain and obvious: He pays attention, monitoring sail shape, boat speed, boat motion, and position. He watches the wind. He notices small shifts, sees them coming and going so keenly non-sailors might think he has a pipeline to Aeolus. He trims sail by cause and effect, not by rote or rule. He always makes the boat go faster and, more important to my way of thinking, feel better. Seeing the wind *is* sailing.

Not surprisingly, *Plain Sailing* is written in clear prose that's laced with humor and understanding. Murphy is a professional writer, not a professional sailor, and that works to the reader's advantage. He's never cynical, never condescending. He knows that learning to sail is not easy, especially as an adult, and he is not cavalier with sailing's specialized lingo. Yet he never dumbs things down. He respects your intellect and your precious time by explaining things exceedingly well. His description of apparent wind and how it differs from true wind, a concept that often bewilders new sailors, is brilliant. His notions of tacking, jibing or otherwise turning a boat follow a logical sequence that focuses not on the technicalities, but on the wind and its angle to the centerline of the boat, which of course makes perfect sense.

Murphy stresses that sailing is sensual, but don't think you're about to read a book of sailing poetry. Murphy is not apologetic about enjoying technical sailing. He wants whatever boat he's aboard, whether it's a one-design racer or my heavy cruising boat, to perform as well as it can. He agonizes if a boat lolls along with poorly trimmed sails and inefficient helming. It's as if his friend, the wind, is reprimanding him. He is a technical sailor—all good sailors are—but he doesn't try to show off his knowledge or skill. Instead, he spells it out plainly, as the title suggests.

Dallas wants you to learn to sail well and confidently, to feel the press of wind in the sails, to respond to the signals from the rudder, and ultimately to appreciate the unique rewards of sailing. I suspect this book may change your life, or at least how you spend your ever-dwindling allotment of time in the boat. Read *Plain Sailing*–find a boat–sail Murphy's way. You'll never regret it; just e-mail Dallas a thank-you note.

John Kretschmer

INTRODUCTION

Sailing is fun, a relaxing diversion from shoreside concerns, a lifelong source of personal satisfaction, accomplishment, and association with elemental nature. What else? Oh, yes, a unique combination of intellectual stimulation and physical exercise. Why, then, do so few new sailors proceed to become experienced sailors, but fade away from the sport before they acquire enough knowledge to appreciate its subtleties, its variety and rewards? There are personal reasons for this: time constraints, shoreside obligations, and things that have nothing to do with sailing per se. Still, though I have no scientific poll to offer, only years of observation, I suspect that part of the reason has directly to do with sailing, specifically the seemingly steep slope of the learning curve right at the beginning.

To a new sailor, a sailboat is an unstable, crowded country where the locals speak gibberish. Everything is unprecedented, esoteric, and slightly intimidating. Sailing seems to make no sense. After two tacks and a jibe, the new sailor gives up on sense and hunches in the corner of the cockpit while experienced guys clamber around pulling on ropes and talking tirelessly about something or other up in the sails. Occasionally a considerate crew member stops by to explain things, but he's still speaking gibberish. Bereft of context as well as language, the new sailor grins vacantly, nodding, hoping he won't be asked to do anything. Then comes a sudden gust of wind, the boat heels sharply, and the new sailor who thought to take up sailing because it might be fun decides to stick with golf.

Admittedly, that may be an exaggeration, but it's none to say that low-grade anxiety, confusion, and a degree of intimidation are common feelings among fledgling sailors. There is no dry-land precedent to bring to the sport—as when a good shortstop takes up tennis, for instance, and the moves feel familiar. The new sailor doesn't even speak the language, so there's no way to know what's coming next. Factor water into the mix, the medium people drown in, and confusion and disorientation sometimes add up to apprehension. What if this thing just turns over? What's to stop it?

Those esoteric bits and barbs, the hardware and the ropes and things with arcane names—they all contribute to confusion. But the central reason why new sailors are confused is that they are utterly unused to thinking about or even noticing wind. Yet wind is the grammar, the organizing principle behind sailing. Wind determines absolutely everything except the kind of sandwiches aboard. Where is the wind? That is the prime question in sailing. Sailing will make no sense until the new sailor learns to make sense of the wind. But wind is often the last thing the new, distracted, and confused sailor focuses on. This book, like its subject, will use wind as its ordering principle, and in it I will repeatedly stress wind awareness.

If you're thinking of buying your first boat or planning to take up sailing in order to sail on other people's boats; if you've enrolled in or have just completed a short sailing course; or if you're looking for a refresher after a long time ashore—then this may be just the book for you. I will have nothing to say about navigation, anchoring techniques, docking procedures, open-ocean sailing, or heavy-weather tactics. The subject here is plain sailing, the interaction between wind and sails, with the aim of understanding how and why you trim a sail to make maximum use of wind power. I will only skirt the edges of the physics of sailing, force-vectors and things like that, for instance, not because they're unimportant, but because the weight of their explanation often overcomes their usefulness to a new sailor. That said, this must also be said: Sailing is technical. There is no getting around that, nor should there be, even at the basic level. I'll try, in *Plain Sailing*, to speed the learning process by focusing exclusively on the sails and on their relationship to moving air. Manually adjusting the sails to make the most efficient use of wind in order to go where you want to go—that's sail trim. Those technical things with esoteric names are essential as devices that actually adjust sails, but all the moves are determined by the wind.

I wish I could tell you honestly that this book will eliminate onboard unease in the early learning stage. I wish I could tell that you'll know how to trim sails after you read this book, to tack and jibe with certainty, precision, and safety. I wouldn't, I can't. I can discuss how and, always, why you trim the sails; I can explain the techniques for tacking and jibing. And I can offer encouragement—you'll discover that it really isn't very hard to sail. It's just the early stage—when everything aboard is foreign and obscure—that's hard, but it's a brief period if you put in time in the boat. Sailing is in fact fun, relaxing, a diversion from shoreside concerns, a lifelong source of personal satisfaction, accomplishment, and association with elemental nature. Furthermore, sailing can reach out and grab a person and hold on for a lifetime. Not always, but it does happen, so be warned.

PLAIN
SAILING

1
———

GETTING STARTED
IN SAILING

AILING—SPECIFICALLY HOW YOU CHOOSE TO SAIL—is a matter of self-expression, and there are a lot of ways to express yourself. I sail sometimes with people interested only in traditional wooden boats, who dismiss as an ugly travesty anything built after 1975 and anything built of fiberglass anytime. It seems natural to them to put up with the leaks, the cost, and the constant maintenance wooden boats require. The pleasure and beauty and tradition in wood make up for its demands on time and checking account. I sail with other people for whom sailing and racing are synonymous. They just don't get why anyone would want to go cruising. Boring.

I for one took up sailing with lingering childhood dreams of long, eventful voyages to reef-ringed tropical islands, exquisite anchorages in azure lagoons; that was real sailing. Later (and still) my ambitions shifted to high-latitude wilderness cruising. While I was still getting started in the sport, I accepted an invitation to join a friend's racing crew. He needed a main trimmer. I knew how to sail, but I didn't know how to trim a main in a race. Yet I reasoned that, though I wasn't interested in short-course racing, I could learn a thing or two that would benefit me when heading for Greenland. I was soon captivated by racing, not for the competition per se, but for the focus on technical sailing, the challenge of getting the most out of the sails, the constant focus on the wind, the very things that some sailors consider too much hassle. And I liked, also, the teamwork, the synchronization of tasks, the camaraderie. I liked the concerted talk about sailing after the race was done. This, too, was sailing. And it did indeed help me when sailing offshore in all weathers. And as for today, sailing on a sunny August Saturday, I'm happy to drop the hook and have a picnic—anytime.

This is to suggest that you go learn the basics, leaving ashore for now your preconceptions about the sort of sailing you think you want to pursue later. Or if you have no preconceptions, only the vague idea that sailing will be fun, better still. In any case, you'll need to learn the basics. I hope this book is useful in that respect, but neither this nor any other manual will serve unless you get in a boat and actually sail. That being the necessary objective, let's look at the various ways you can acquire on-the-water experience.

If you own or are buying a boat, then you'll have plenty of opportunity to practice anytime and any way you wish. However, you don't need to own a boat to get started in sailing. I've been sailing seriously for more than thirty years, yet I've never owned a boat or belonged to any kind of club. I don't say that that's necessarily a good thing, only that it can be done. I'd probably buy a boat if money were no object, and yacht clubs are pleasing places where people with common interests gather and around which some members construct a major segment of their social lives. I would have applied to join a club if membership were a prerequisite to sailing, but it's not. For the likes of me, yacht clubs are pleasing places where other people keep their boats. And in case you were wondering, the old cliché of the snooty yacht club where you'll be looked down on by guys in red pants and blue blazers with fouled anchors embroidered on their breast pockets if your direct relatives didn't sail over on the *Mayflower* is antique. Sure, there are still exclusive clubs with some puffed-up, snooty members of the type you don't want anything to do with, but the same could probably be said of the PTA.

Further, you don't need to live within easy commute to an arm of the sea. People are sailing actively—and very well—on lakes and rivers throughout this and other countries. There are no social, financial, or geographical impediments to prevent you from getting started in sailing.

SAILING SCHOOLS

The US Sailing Association certifies sailing schools across the country as well as being a highly valuable resource for all aspects of sailing (http://us-sailing.org/training). Steve and Doris Colgate's Offshore Sailing School, Annapolis Sailing School, J World, and the Blue Water Sailing School are among the larger organized schools with professional franchises all over the country. The owners and instructors have thought long and hard about the pedagogy and the on-water techniques for teaching total beginners how to sail. These and other schools all offer courses of various lengths, cost, and focus (basic sailing, cruising, racing). You can enroll in private or group courses near your home or in various "vacation destinations." Colgate, for example, has three locations in Florida, two in New York, as well as Tortola, St. Martin, and the Chesapeake. J World, which Practical Sailor, the Consumer Reports of the sailing industry, ranked as the best in the country, has schools in Annapolis, Key West, Newport, San Diego, and San Francisco.

Also, there are numerous local, private sailing schools from coast to coast. Some are specialized; for instance, check www.womanship.com, an excellent organization founded on the principle that women more readily learn to sail when their fellow students and their instructors are women. While it's true that more men than women sail actively and own boats, the view that sailing is dominated by a bunch of sweaty guys drinking beer and shouting at one another is also an antique cliché. Speaking as a man, I don't sail with idiots, at least not twice. You'll find semi-civilized brutes in all activities, but by and large women are welcomed aboard sailboats and accorded all due courtesy and respect. And if you—male or female—don't like the people you're sailing with, find another boat to sail on. That won't be difficult.

If you're thinking of sailing as a family endeavor, you'll find youth sailing programs at every yacht club and organized teaching facility as well as many community-sponsored training programs.

There is usually someone around yacht and sailing clubs with a sideline job teaching new sailors, a kind of coach who, for a reasonable fee, will be pleased to go sailing with you and help you learn the finer points. This suggests a broad point about getting started in sailing: Visit, hang around places like clubs and marinas where they keep boats, get to know the people, ask for suggestions. Someone is very likely to invite you aboard his or her boat. As a rule, people who sail like to help people who want to learn to sail.

RACING

You may find that the racing ethos is simply not for you, something diametrically opposite to the tranquil ideal of sailing. However, there is a lot of misconception about sailboat racing. A friend recently bought a Tartan Ten, a fine, inexpensive 30-foot production boat with active racing fleets throughout the country. But he refuses to consider racing, even at the most informal level, because some rude owner shouted at him—twenty years ago. Mention racing, and he'll do fifteen minutes on racers as unhinged, testosterone-crazed hysterics. We've all found ourselves at one time or another crewing for a guy who seemed sensible and civilized at the dock, only to reveal his Captain Bligh complex as soon as the starting gun fired—but not twice. Besides, bad behavior is not endemic to sailboat racing. Some parents watching their kid's Little League baseball games turn into crazies you want to flee from.

There are several advantages to racing during the early stages of your sailing education. The first and most valuable is that you will likely find a "ride" very quickly. There may be no place for the beginner aboard serious race boats in the bigger regattas or on a dinghy with only two or three crew. And some crews are like families. However, most racing—in terms of the number of participants—takes place at the local club level aboard cruiser-racers, dual-purpose boats in the 30- to 40-foot range with a galley, head, and furniture below, not flat-out, stripped-down, dedicated race boats staffed by hotshots. All sailboats, fast or slow, big or small, can race against one another under a rating system known as the Performance Handicap Racing Fleet that seeks to equalize the performance of dissimilar boats by ascribing handicaps to the faster, bigger boats.

Almost every yacht club in the country runs a midweek evening race series with a start time around 7. And some, if not many, boat owners race only on weeknights, using their boat for family cruising on the weekends.

The weeknight race is an excellent venue both to gain on-water experience and to learn whether racing is for you. You don't need to be a member of the club to participate.

Back to that most encouraging aspect of racing for the new sailor—you are needed. The typical 35-foot cruiser-racer needs six to eight crew to sail competitively. Thus, it's in the vested interest of racing organizations to encourage and welcome new blood. At most yacht clubs, you'll find a bulletin board spattered with CREW WANTED signs, and the club's Website will post similar calls. For crew, even inexperienced crew, it's a seller's market. And this is especially true for weeknight racing at the local club level. There will be a core group of several experienced regulars aboard the typical cruiser-racer—helmsman, trimmers, bow person—and the remainder are needed as movable ballast to keep the boat sailing flat.

"What?" you might ask. "Why would I want to do that? I'm not taking up sailing to be ballast on a tippy boat." Well, because there are advantages to racing as a mode of education.

Racing is total immersion in pure sailing. There should be no idle conversations on race boats—chatting is for daysailing and cruising. The talk is only of the wind, sails, maneuvers, and the other boats. As a new sailor, you won't have much to contribute about wind shifts, sail changes, or port-tack crossing situations. But you will before too long, if you put in the time; and at the outset you can race with no need for performance anxiety. Ride the windward rail for a while; see if you like racing and the people you're racing with. If you pay attention even when you're not doing anything and evince an interest in learning, you will be noticed—and valued. Before long you will be asked to take on a more active role in making the boat go fast. In most areas of the country, you could, if you wanted to, race every Wednesday evening and every weekend of the season. Also, you will meet a lot of sailors, thus broadening your sailing alternatives.

But in fairness to race boat owners, we should look at you, the new sailor, from their perspective. The owner is not in need of the occasional crew who'll show up for the ride when it's convenient. The typical cruiser-racer owner is looking for regular, dependable crew. He's trying to build a team. She'll willingly settle for the inexperienced crew if she can depend on your presence. To phone an owner more than once at 3 PM and say you can't make it tonight is a sailing faux pas.

But by all means give racing a chance as a means to gain quick experience. Concentrate on the pure sailing. There usually isn't time for crew or owners to explain why they're tacking sooner than later or how they're calling the wind shifts, but it's very good exercise to try to figure it out for yourself—and talk about it after the race. Besides, you may find racing, the camaraderie and the excitement, to be fun, not stressful. If you don't like the owner and his crew, then politely withdraw and find another boat. In many areas, you can find an entirely different club within 15 miles of the first. And of course if you discover you don't want to race, then don't. There are other ways to gain experience.

CHARTERING

Anywhere you find a significant body of water, you will find a charter operation. Some charters come with a captain; some are bareboat, meaning you're the captain. Among the big names are TMM, the Moorings, and Sunsail, with franchises in the Caribbean, the Med, the Adriatic, the tropical Pacific, and all points in between. (A quick Google search of "bareboat charters" turned up 149,000 entries.) The larger operators and many of the smaller have chartering down to a science. Competition is intense, and the names mentioned above, along with many others, are highly vested in your having a good time. In many of the most popular charter destinations—the Virgin Islands, for instance—the sailing is easy, winds steady, water uniformly deep, and numerous beautiful anchorages on different islands lie within sight of one another. Operators in these places, while they won't charter a boat to someone who knows nothing, can afford to accept people of limited experience. In some other areas, such as the coast of Maine, where the sailing is more challenging (fog, strong currents, granite bottom), charterers will look more carefully at your résumé.

If of course you choose a captained charter, your experience level does not matter. Chances are highly likely, again given intense competition, that your captain will be a congenial human being, as well as an expert boat driver, quite willing to teach if you express an interest in learning. And many operators offer a half-captained, half-bareboat charter. The captain comes along during, say, the first three days of your charter to help you get acquainted with the boat and the waters; then you drop him off somewhere and continue on your own.

Today you can charter literally anywhere in the world, from Antarctica to Greenland, with experienced captains. Though wilderness and high-latitude chartering has been around for the last couple of decades, many sailors remain unaware of the possibilities. For instance, Pelagic Expeditions and Expedition Sail offer charters to the Falklands, South Georgia, Cape Horn, and the Antarctic Peninsula. A one-man operation, John Kretschmer Sailing, which charters in the Med during the summer and the Caribbean in winter, makes two transatlantic crossings per year and offers blue-water passages of various lengths and locales to charterers, no previous experience necessary.

To put it succinctly, it's easy to get started in sailing; I've listed only the most conventional means. You'll find others, perhaps online or by asking around at work or in social circles. If you want to sail, there is nothing to stop you.

SAFETY

Sailing is a safe sport. It's a bit politically incorrect to put it that way, since such a bald statement might seem to imply that you needn't concern yourself with safety. It doesn't imply that. And you do need to concern yourself with safety. Though an extended disquisition on safety is beyond the province of this book, I'll make some general statements in a later chapter and refer you to sources of safety information and to professionally staffed workshops on safety. Suffice it to say, for now, that serious or fatal accidents are rare in sailing, far rarer than in other segments of boating such as canoeing and personal watercraft operation. This is not a statistical coincidence. Just to make a sailboat go where you want it to requires more experience and knowledge than, say, a PWC on which you need only twist the throttle to go fast. Far and away most of the accidents that occur on the water, regardless of the vessel, result from carelessness and stupidity. Therefore, the application of common sense will prevent most accidents. And time in the boat—experience—will alleviate vague anxiety.

So for now, let the goal be to get yourself on a sailboat. Obviously, that will be easy if you're a new owner, but it won't be difficult if you're not. This spring, while I was sanding the bottom of our little race boat with other crew, we overheard a bright young couple talking to the owner of a nearby boat. The couple, new to sailing, were introducing themselves, expressing their interest, their willingness to learn, and their commitment to showing up. We had a full crew, but not everyone can make every Wednesday-night race, so we're always on the lookout for new blood. We ceased sanding, glanced at one another, and nodded. As soon as the conversation next door ended, our owner approached the couple. Did they want to race?

"Well, sure," the man said. "But we never have."

"That's okay." Our owner whipped out his BlackBerry to record the couple's e-mail address. "I'll be in touch."

At that moment, I'm certain, similar arrangements were being made from San Francisco Bay to the Gulf of Maine. You are wanted and welcomed. All you need do is show up with a willingness to learn.

2

LANGUAGE

PUT SEVERAL SAILORS TOGETHER ON A BOAT or in a yacht club bar and they'll blather sentence after sentence without uttering a single noun or verb commonly understood by nonsailors. Broach, roach, vang, tang, tack, jibe, leech, luff, clew, halyard, outhaul. Nonsense to the uninitiated, some of whom I've heard voice the suspicion that sailors talk that way because they're a lot of rich, snooty types happy to keep the hoi polloi on the far side of the language divide. Not so.

Sailors talk like that because they must. Sailing, though highly evolved, is literally an ancient technology. Most of the nouns and verbs that express it are the same used by sailors three centuries before anyone ever imagined there would be something called a yacht club or that people would sail for recreation, for fun, for heaven's sake. Common, dry-land language cannot suffice on sailboats because of the highly specialized nature of sailing. Consider the humble boom vang, a mainsail control found on all boats.

"Please ease the vang," says the skipper to his crew.

"The what?"

"That blue rope leading from the thing connecting the bottom of the boom to the base of the mast."

"This?"

"No, no, the other blue rope."

That kind of communication won't work. Nothing else does what a boom vang does, so it has to be named. The same applies to sheets and topping lifts, backstays and Cunninghams. And this brings us to the question of study, of homework. It's probably not too rigid to say that you cannot crack the initial barriers to learning until you know the language. Sure, you can learn as you go, but it takes longer, and your shipmates, growing weary of asking you to pull on the blue line, will not take seriously your commitment to the sport if you consistently need translation. I don't see much alternative to simply memorizing the names of the parts of a boat, its mast, rigging, sails, and the lines that control them as a start.

However, what follows is not a glossary, nor a pure vocabulary lesson. I will let the words that describe hulls, masts, sails, and sail-control lines serve as portals into some of the fundamental principles and realities of sailing. Following this chapter, I'll assume a common understanding of the words. There is no choice. Otherwise I'd be doing the literary equivalent of asking you to pull on the blue rope, no, the other blue rope.

THE HULL

First things first: The simple reason boats float, perhaps their most important characteristic, is because the weight of water displaced by a boat's hull is greater than the weight of the boat and everything aboard. Thus the boat is said to be buoyant. Fully loaded supertankers are buoyant, which gives you an idea of the density of the substance boats have to move through. (Salt water weighs 64 pounds per cubic foot, fresh water 62.2.)

Second, in the broadest sense, all sailboats are the same. They vary widely in size and shape depending on their intended purpose, such as racing, cruising, or daysailing; and within those broad categories, you will find a variety of shapes and sizes depending on the age of the boat, the opinion of its designer, and the changing trends in the marketplace. However, when they change course, when they tack or jibe, the crew aboard a 50-footer perform the same routine as on an 18-foot dinghy. And all the parts—hulls, masts and the standing rigging to support them, sails and sail-control lines—have the same names. If you can sail one boat, you can sail them all because all sailboats avail themselves of the same source of motive power in the same ways.

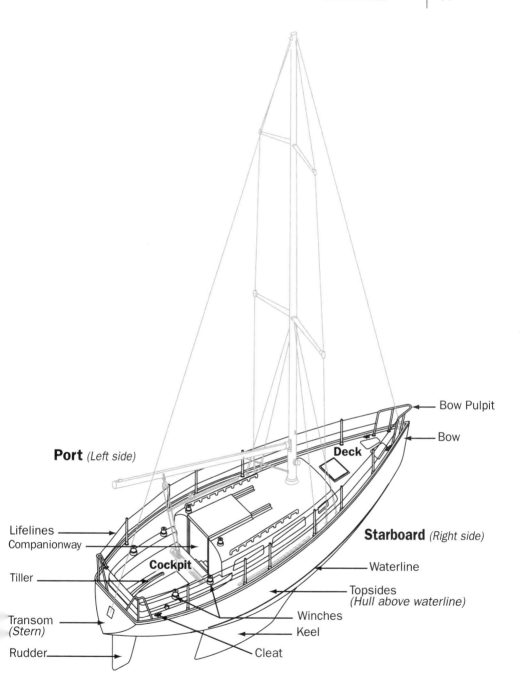

Port *(Left side)*

Deck

Bow Pulpit

Bow

Starboard *(Right side)*

Lifelines

Companionway

Tiller

Cockpit

Transom
(Stern)

Rudder

Winches

Cleat

Keel

Topsides
(Hull above waterline)

Waterline

Illustration © 2009 www.marineillustration.com.

In this book, we'll be concerned mainly with the stuff above the deck, the mast and its rigging, the sails and the lines that control their set and trim. But before we get to the things aloft, let's take a quick tour around the deck to make sure we're speaking the same language. Please study carefully the above illustration for a more complete vocabulary. Let's start in the stern where the steering gear is situated. (By the way, the very aft part of the stern is called the transom.)

Unlike cars, all boats turn by the stern, but it will feel as though the bow is turning first. For new sailors, this results in a tendency to oversteer, which will only be overcome with practice. The rudder is the mechanism that actually turns the boat. When the rudder is turned to the right (to starboard), the water flowing over its surface pushes the stern to the left (to port), and the boat turns to the right. The helm is the mechanism that turns the rudder. In small boats the helm will be a tiller, a simple stick attached to the top of the rudderstock. In that case, rudder and tiller make up a single unit attached to and detachable from the transom, and in fact referred to as a transom-hung rudder. New sailors might find tiller steering confusing at first, because to turn the boat to the right you push the tiller to the left. Again, with practice this move will become second nature, and you'll stop thinking about it in rote terms: "If I push the tiller one way the boat will turn the other way. Hmm."

Larger boats will be helmed with a wheel linked to the rudder by a system of cables and pulleys, and the rudder itself will be part of the underbody of the boat as opposed to a unit hung over the transom. In these boats, the wheel is usually situated at the aft end of the cockpit. Let's start with a walk forward along one side deck or the other. (The reason we say starboard, the right side of the boat as you're facing forward, and port, the left, instead of simply right or left, is that on boats you won't always be facing forward.)

The boat widens as you move forward to the beam, its widest point measured from side to side, or athwartships. The mast is usually placed forward of the beam. And of course the hull and deck taper again toward the bow, the very forward point of which is called the stem. Technically, boats have two bows, a port and starboard. Therefore, you might hear someone say, "I see the buoy just off the starboard bow." Once you pass the mast, you're standing on the foredeck.

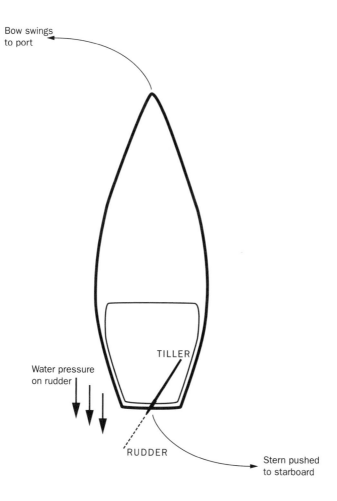

Bow swings
to port

TILLER

Water pressure
on rudder

RUDDER

Stern pushed
to starboard

All sailboats turn by the stern. If you move the rudder over in one direction, the force of water pressure against the rudder will turn the stern in the opposite direction.

Everything below the deck, including the parts above and below the water, is the hull. That part of the hull beneath the water is called the underbody, or sometimes the wetted surface. The bulging sides of the hull beneath the waterline are called the bilges. And that part of the hull between the waterline and the deck is called the topsides.

Now, while you're standing on the foredeck, start looking up. Notice that cabled wire extending from the point of the bow to the top, or near the top, of the mast. This is the headstay. Its job is to support the mast against forces in the sails that want to push the mast backward, or aft. Notice that the headstay has a colleague at the back of the boat, a wire running from the top of the mast to the transom. This is the backstay. Sails, even in rather light wind, exert significant stress on the mast that most could not withstand without additional support. When the wind blows from over the front of the boat, the stress in the sails exerts an aft-ward force on the mast, in which case the headstay helps support the mast. And when the wind blows over the back of the boat, the backstay takes over to support the mast, as common sense would suggest.

But the mast also needs side-to-side, athwartships support. So step aft to one side or the other of the mast and look at the wires stretching from one or more points along the top and sides of the mast down to the side decks. These wires are the shrouds. Though their configuration, their geometry, will vary from boat to boat depending on size, shrouds counteract the lateral forces generated on the mast particularly when sailing to windward—that is, when the wind blows over the front of the boat.

Collectively, the stays and shrouds constitute the standing rigging.

All pieces of the standing rigging are attached to the deck with adjustable turnbuckles. In most boats, the tension on each is generally drawn up tight to keep the mast straight up and down. I'll have more to say later about rig tension, but for now keep in the back of your mind the fact that on some boats tightening or loosening the standing rigging will bend or straighten the mast, and that in turn will affect the shape of the sails.

Now that we have it supported fore and aft (headstay and backstay) as well as athwartships (shrouds), let's have a look at the mast itself. In sailing, you'll spend a lot of time looking up.

MASTS AND MAST WORDS

The obvious basic purpose of the mast is to hold up the sails, but a glance around any mooring field will show that all masts are not created equal, even those on similar-sized boats. Some masts are short and stubby, while others tower over the deck. Some are as stout as bridge abutments, others beanpole-thin. A mom-and-pop cruising boat 34 feet long will naturally carry less sail area on a shorter, stouter mast than a 34-foot dedicated race boat meant to carry movable ballast in the form of human bodies.

The number and spatial configuration of masts constitute a boat's rig. There are four different rigs most commonly seen on sailboats today. Ketches and yawls, among the more traditional rigs, sport two masts, the larger mainmast forward, the smaller mizzenmast stepped aft. The actual position of the mizzen, whether it's mounted forward of the rudder shaft (ketch) or aft (yawl), distinguishes one from the other. You'll also see cat-boats (not to be confused with catamarans) with a single mast stepped right up at the bow and a single, large sail. Far and away, however, the most common rig today is the sloop. Sloops carry one mast with two sails, a mainsail and one headsail.

Every rig has its devoted following, and before long you will hear out-landish claims about their relative superiority. Time and technology (which often flow from racing to the cruising sailor) have shown, however, that when pure sailing performance is the criterion, the sloop is the most efficient rig. The reason why—the efficient flow of wind around and between the two sails—is essentially the subject of this book, and in it we will focus exclusively on sloops, while appreciating the certain advantages and pleasingly salty appearance of ketches, yawls, and catboats.

The height of the mast and the length of the boom determine the size of the mainsail in square-foot area; and the relative length of the mast and boom (collectively called spars) determine the shape of the mainsail. The thinner and taller the mast, the more standing rigging you need to support it, along with the additional hardware required to attach shrouds and stays to the mast and deck. That's the disadvantage of a light, thin mast. The advantage—and it's a big one—to a light mast is that it's light. It's a basic law of sailing that when it blows from over the front of the boat, most of the wind's force wants to push the boat onto its side, or in proper language to cause it to heel. Once a boat starts to heel, the weight of the mast causes it to heel

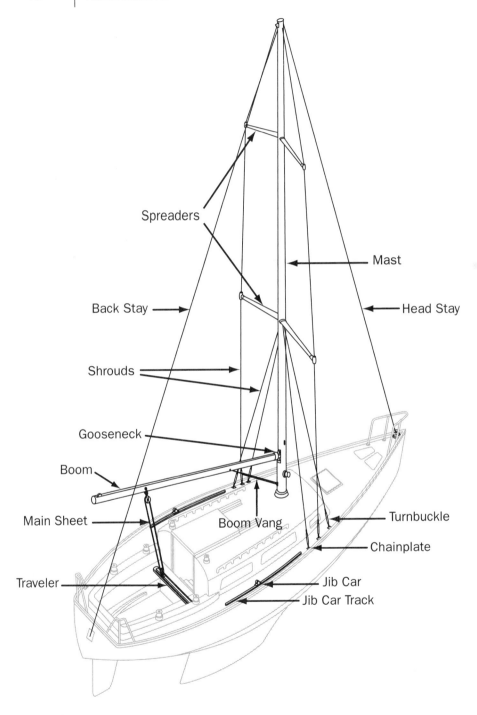

Spreaders

Mast

Back Stay

Head Stay

Shrouds

Gooseneck

Boom

Main Sheet

Boom Vang

Turnbuckle

Chainplate

Traveler

Jib Car

Jib Car Track

Illustration © 2009 www.marineillustration.com.

farther, and the heavier the mast, the greater the heeling force. Heeling beyond a certain small angle is undesirable. Not only is it uncomfortable and precarious to live at an angle, but when a boat heels too much, it begins to slide sideways, or make leeway, instead of going forward. Since each pound of weight is magnified many times in effect as it climbs up the mast, weight aloft is the enemy of fast, efficient sailing.

As you peer up the mast, notice those appendages protruding horizontally perpendicular to the mast. These are called spreaders because that's what they do—they spread the load on the mast. Picture a tall radio tower and the shroud-like guy wires that support it. The farther from the base of the tower you can anchor the wires, the greater the support they will afford. But of course on a sailboat, the shrouds can't be anchored any farther outboard than the width of the beam. Spreaders serve to compensate for that necessarily narrow shroud base. Really tall, thin masts on hotshot race boats in the 45-foot range might require as many as five spreaders. (I sailed with a guy in a lovely traditional boat with a single-spreader rig who, as we sailed out of Newport, Rhode Island's harbor, home of hotshot race boats, admitted to a twinge of "spreader envy.")

THE SAILS

If you stick with the sport, you will develop an intimacy with sails. But to the new sailor, sails are the things that make sailing hard. Yes, but sails are the things that make sailing interesting, as well as possible. Try to see them in those terms from your earliest introduction. Modern sailmakers have turned this ancient, simple device into a highly sophisticated, richly subtle aeronautical instrument. You can make today's sails do remarkable things, and the range of possibilities is great enough that no sailor ever stops learning about sails.

As we discuss the language of sails, please bear in mind that the sailmaker designs into them an aerodynamic shape; no modern sail is a flat piece of material. But unlike airplane wings, to which sails are often compared, our sails need to operate efficiently in a wide range of conditions and angular relations to the wind. Trim is about adjusting the shape and angle of the sails to maintain efficient forward movement in light air and heavy air, when the wind blows over the bow of the boat, the beam, stern, and all points in between.

That said, let's hoist the sails and have a look at them. It doesn't matter what boat you're on, and since there is no wind, we're not going anywhere just yet. So you won't be able to see that curve your sailmaker has designed into the sails, but we can have a look at their parts, for now, in order to establish our common language. Let's begin with the mainsail, it being the one you'll usually set first.

When not in use, the main is usually folded, or flaked, on the boom and held there with sail ties. Remove the ties, and then attach the halyard to the head of the sail. Halyards hoist sails, so all sailboats must have halyards. They are attached, usually with a metal shackle, to the upper corner of the sail, the head. Since they are triangles, all modern sails have three corners:

The forward lower corner is the tack. The clew is the lower, aft corner of the sail, and of course the head is the upper corner. If the main is flaked on the boom when not in use, then the tack is already attached at the intersection of mast and boom, or the gooseneck. Likewise, the clew is already attached to the after end of the boom. (Dinghy and other small-boat owners like to remove the mainsail at the end of a day's sailing, roll it up, and stow it below for safekeeping, but this isn't practical in bigger boats with large mains.)

So you've attached the halyard to the head of the main. The halyard must of course run to the top of the mast over a pulley, and then come back down, usually inside the mast, to a point near the deck within reach. Some halyards are attached to the mast, some are led aft to the cockpit, but it doesn't matter. You still pull down on the halyard to hoist the sail. Notice how the front part of the mainsail runs up the mast in a groove at the back of the mast. Tension the halyard enough to remove wrinkles in the front of the sail. After you tie off the halyard (to keep the sail up), step back and have a look at the mainsail.

Being a triangle, it also has three edges:

The forward or leading edge, the one attached to the mast, is the luff.

The aft part of the sail is called the leech.

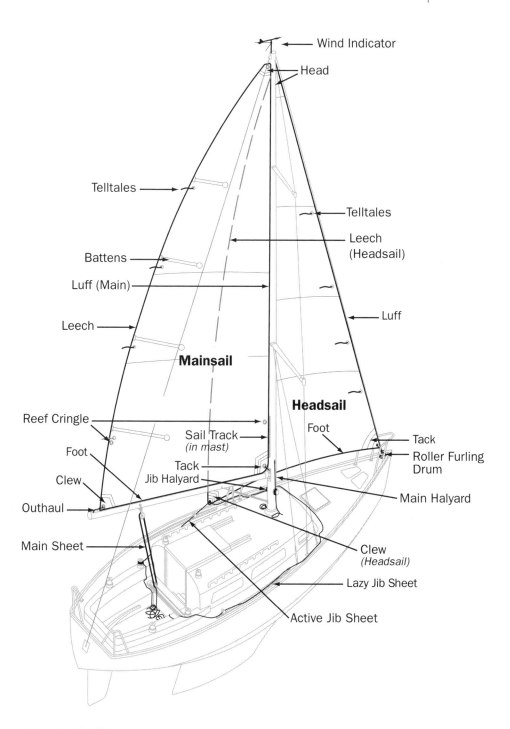

Wind Indicator

Head

Telltales

Telltales

Leech
(Headsail)

Battens

Luff (Main)

Luff

Leech

Mainsail

Headsail

Reef Cringle

Foot

Sail Track
(in mast)

Tack

Foot

Tack

Roller Furling
Drum

Clew

Jib Halyard

Main Halyard

Outhaul

Main Sheet

Clew
(Headsail)

Lazy Jib Sheet

Active Jib Sheet

Illustration © 2009 www.marineillustration.com.

The mainsail is a right triangle with the leech as the hypotenuse. However, if you draw an imaginary line from the head of the main down to the clew, you will notice an arc of cloth extending beyond that line. This is the roach. Without a roach, there would be no fair curve at the back of the main. Instead of flowing smoothly, the wind would grow turbulent as it flows off the back of the main. Further, the roach acts a kind of rudder when you're sailing to windward. You don't need to understand how this works—I'll have much to say later about airflow over the sails—for now just grasp the language.

Because the roach extends beyond the hypotenuse, it needs some additional support to maintain the desirable curve. That's what battens do, flat strips of some stiff material such as fiberglass, nylon, or carbon fiber inserted into horizontal pockets sewn into the leech of the main. Some battens are short, only about twice as long as the roach itself. Others run the length of the sail from leech to luff; these are called full-length battens, often shortened to full battens.

The bottom of the sail is called, logically for once, the foot. The foot of the mainsail is sometimes fixed to the boom by means of a boltrope running in a groove in the boom. In that case, the sailmaker adds extra cloth to the foot, called the shelf, which allows the foot to curve when the outhaul is eased. There is a trend today toward "loose-footed" mainsails attached only at the tack and clew with a flap of loose cloth hanging over the boom. This is lighter and cheaper, and it allows for a wider range of adjustments.

Since there is no wind, we can leave the mainsail up. Now let's turn to the headsail. The names of its corners (tack, clew, head) and its edges (luff, leech, foot) are the same as the mainsail. But the headsail is a relatively simpler sail than the main, primarily because it does not require a boom. Its foot runs free, as it must, since the sail must be pulled from one side of the boat to the other with each tack and jibe. Another difference between headsail and mainsail has to do with their leading edges, their luffs. The luff of the main is affixed in a groove running up the aft side of the mast. But there is only a wire, the headstay, to accommodate the luff of the headsail. So in our imaginary sail inspection, we can't merely say, "Okay, now let's hoist the headsail," until we determine the means by which its leading edge, its luff, is attached to the headstay. There are two:

If the boat is a dinghy or a small keelboat, the luff of the headsail will be attached to the headstay by spring-loaded clips, properly called hanks. After a day's sailing, small-boat headsails are usually detached from the headstay and stored below, which means that you will have bring the sail topside to the foredeck, attach the tack to a dedicated fitting at the base of the headstay, and then one by one clip the hanks to the wire. That done, you then tie the sheets, those lines that control the trim, to the clew of the sail. All that remains is to clip the halyard to the head of the sail—and hoist.

If it is a larger boat, one, say, in excess of 26 feet, chances are the headsail will already be hoisted and rolled around the headstay on a roller-furling device. The roller furler has done more than any other single device to make sailing simpler, easier, and cheaper. The system consists of a thin aluminum extrusion fitted around the headstay from bottom to top. The extrusion forms a groove (like that in the mast). A boltrope sewn into the luff of the headsail slides into the groove. At deck level, this long extrusion is connected to a small drum around which the furling line is wound. The furling line is then led aft along the side deck to some convenient place in the cockpit, and cleated.

Hauling on the furling line turns the drum and the attached extrusion spins around the headstay and thus rolls sail around and around the headstay in a neat, tight furl. Then to unroll the sail—to set it—all you need to do is uncleat the furling line and pull on one or the other sheet.

The system offers enormous advantages. It allows you to leave the headsail hoisted and rolled when the boat is not in use, particularly convenient on bigger boats with heavy headsails. And in the old days before roller furling, if the wind piped up requiring a smaller headsail, crew would have to haul the new sail onto the (pitching, wet) foredeck, unhank the bigger sail, hank on the smaller one, and reconnect the halyard before hoisting the new sail. Then, still on the foredeck, the crew would have to fold the old sail and either lug it below or lash it to the lifelines. Now, for most recreational sailing, you need only the single headsail. If the wind pipes up requiring smaller sail area, all you need to do is roll in a portion of the headsail by hauling on the furling line. Some degree of sail-shape efficiency will be sacrificed as you shorten the headsail by this means, but it's generally worth it. And by the way, the roller furler is one of the only bits of sailing technology that migrated from cruising boats to race boats, rather than the other way around. Some classes of race boats are now required by the rules to carry one headsail on a roller furler in order to lessen the cost to owners of carrying multiple headsails and therefore giving the advantage to the owners with the fattest wallet.

That said, let's set the headsail and compare it with the mainsail, both of which on our imaginary boat will be hanging limply. Headsail is a collective term, but the specific names vary according to the size of the sail. There is a technical consideration here related to the length of an imaginary line drawn from the clew to the midpoint of the luff. But let's skip that and look at the names of the headsails from a simpler and almost-as-accurate standard. Consider the distance from the foot of the headstay to the front of the mast. Called the fore triangle, its length varies of course according to the size of the boat, but all sloops have a fore triangle. Small headsails that operate within the fore triangle are designated as 100 percent. Larger ones, when the foot and leech overlap the mast, are called genoas, but not all genoas are equal in size. Their size is designated by the distance of that overlap stated in percentage of distance greater than the length of the fore triangle. For instance, if the genoa overlaps—that is, extends aft of the mast—by half the length of the fore triangle, it is designated a 150 percent genoa, or simply a 150. That's about as big as genoas get, only practical in light air when sailing hard into the wind; and they are a pain to drag around the front of the mast on each tack or jibe. For that reason, standard genoas tend be 135s, a usually happy compromise between too big and too small.

However, in common usage, sailors generally refer to headsails, regardless of size and percentage of overlap, as "jibs." I'd like to adopt the usage, recognizing that when we say "jibs," we're talking about 100 percent jibs, 150 percent genoas, and all in between; I'll differentiate when necessary.

In most older boats and some new ones, the headsail will be larger in square-foot area than the mainsail. It will afford, therefore, greater motive power than the main when the boat is sailing with the wind forward of the beam. The headsail will also be more efficient than the mainsail because it operates in undisturbed air out in front of the boat with nothing but a thin wire between the luff and the wind. The wind flow over the main will not be as clean, because the main is set behind the mast. But as we proceed, we'll see that the increased efficiency of the sloop rig results from the interaction of both sails working together. Making them work together is part of the definition and the objective of sail trim, and so we'll cover it in detail. For now, however, in order to make sure we're speaking the same language, let's have a look at the lines that control the trim of the sails.

SAIL-CONTROL LINES

Sails are controlled by ropes. But in proper usage, a "rope" becomes a "line" when it is in use. All sailboats from 15-foot dinghies to 150-foot megayachts require the same lines to control their sails, and all the lines have the same names. The only difference among the various boats is the placement of those lines. So the first thing to do when you go aboard any boat is to "learn the ropes." Pay attention to details, difficult during your early learning stages, since all these lines and systems will tend to blur. Avoid that tendency by studiously isolating one line from the others. Follow it with your eyes and imagine where the lines will go and what they need to do when the sails are hoisted. Each line has two important points along its length. One end will always be attached to the sail or, in the case of the mainsail, to the boom. The other end—the one you pull on—must be "led" and finally positioned somewhere within convenient reach. Recognizing the necessity of that—one end of each line connected to the sail, the other end going somewhere on the boat so that you can conveniently tighten or ease it—will help you sort out specific lines and understand their function. To forestall confusion, most sailors use different-color lines.

HALYARDS

Halyards hoist sails. This means, of course, that one end of the halyard must always be attached to the head of the sail. But the position of the other end varies from boat to boat. Check out your jib halyard. If it goes up to hoist the sail, then the other end has to come down. But where?

In order to streamline the mast, halyards usually run inside the mast from the top and exit through a cutout above deck level, thence to some attachment point. On small boats such as dinghies, the attachment point is a simple cleat mounted on the side of the mast. On larger boats with heavier sails, a winch often mounted on the side of the mast replaces the cleat. The custom today, even on relatively small boats, is to lead the "tail" of the halyard through a turning block near the base of the mast and aft along the deck to a winch mounted on the cabin top. The purpose of this more complicated arrangement is to avoid the necessity for someone to leave the cockpit when setting or dousing the sails. The same applies to main halyards. The tail will either be fixed at the mast or led aft to the cockpit. As with all things sailing, there are advantages and disadvantages to both halyard placements. But never mind; the important point for you at this early stage is to figure out where the tails of the halyards are positioned.

SHEETS

Sheets control the angle at which the sails meet the wind; it's called angle of attack, a term borrowed from aviation. In the coarsest terms, when the wind is forward of the beam, you tighten the sails by hauling on the sheets in order to bring the sails toward the centerline of the boat. Conversely, when the wind meets the sails from aft of the beam, the sheets must be eased. Simple.

JIB SHEETS

Jib sheets are tied directly to the clew using that most valuable of knots, the bowline. (Get yourself a knot book or Google "knots," and teach yourself to tie a bowline. It's vital to sailing.) On bigger boats, with their larger-diameter sheets, the knots are replaced with metal shackles. All headsails need two sheets, the tails of which are led around either side of the mast and aft to winches in the cockpit. On a big genoa, the sheets are led aft outboard of the shrouds, while on a 100% jib, the sheets will probably be led inboard of the shrouds. But only one sheet is working at any one time. For instance, on starboard tack, that is, when the wind is blowing over the starboard bow, the portside sheet is active, actually pulling on the jib clew, since the sail will be drawing on that side of the boat. (In other words, the headsail will always be drawing on the leeward, the downwind side of the boat.) The other sheet,

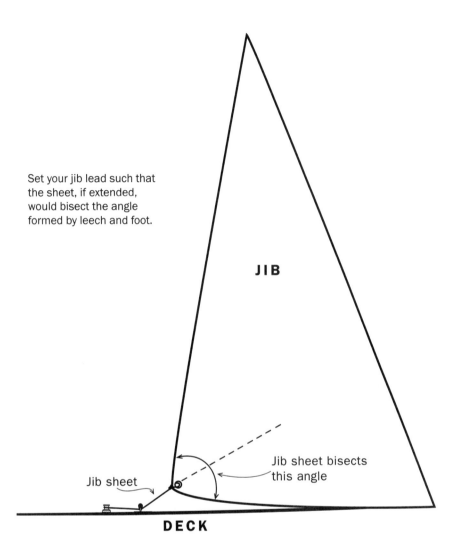

Set your jib lead such that the sheet, if extended, would bisect the angle formed by leech and foot.

JIB

Jib sheet bisects this angle

Jib sheet

DECK

the lazy sheet, lies limply along the windward side of the boat doing nothing until it's time to tack or jibe.

But notice as you follow the jib sheets aft that they pass through a roller or pulley on either side before reaching the cockpit. This is called the jib-sheet lead. The placement of the lead determines the direction of pull on the clew of jib. In order for the jib to draw efficiently, the sheet must pull evenly on two parts of the sail—the foot and the leech. Say you tied your jib sheet to the clew and then ran the sheet directly aft to the cockpit without passing the line through a lead. In that case, you'd have plenty of tension on the foot of the sail, but none on the leech. It would sag away to leeward, spilling wind from the middle and upper parts of the sail. In the opposite extreme, if you position the lead directly below the jib clew, you can exert plenty of

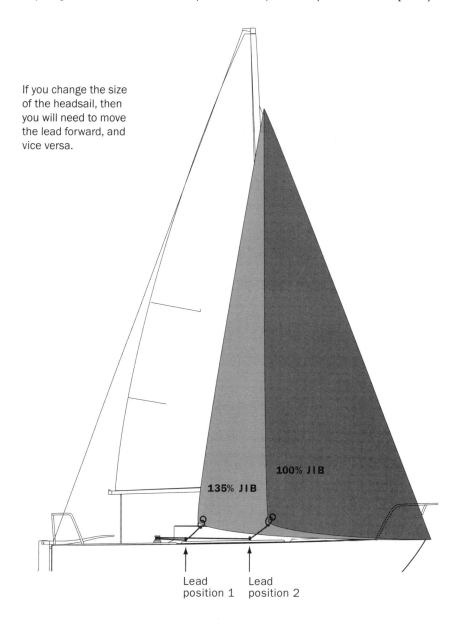

If you change the size of the headsail, then you will need to move the lead forward, and vice versa.

100% JIB

135% JIB

Lead position 1   Lead position 2

downward pull on the leech, but none on the foot. No, you have to set your lead—the lead block is fixed to a track bolted to the deck so that the lead can be moved as necessary—such that it exerts equal down and aft tension. So how do you know where to position the lead in order to split the difference, thus attaining equal pull on the foot and the leech?

Position the lead such that the sheet seems to bisect the angle formed by the foot and the leech.

Often the sailmaker sews a strip of reinforcement material against the stresses on the clew that also bisects the angle for you. Set your lead such that your sheet and the reinforcement strip form a straight line. Now you have a proper basic lead position: The sheet pulls down and aft, producing equal tension on both the foot and the leech.

However, if you change the size of the headsail, as for instance when the wind pipes up and you want to shorten your headsail from 135 to 100 percent, you will also have to change the lead position. If you're shortening sail, then you will have to move the lead forward, and vice versa. The lead position depends mostly on the size of the headsail. But you might also want to adjust the lead position to change the shape of the headsail according to wind conditions. In light air, for instance, you want a full sail obtained by moving the lead slightly forward. As the wind freshens, as boatspeed increases, you may want to move the lead a bit aft, thus flattening the sail. More about that later.

MAINSHEETS

Mainsheets run between a point at or near the aft end of the boom to a point near the centerline of the boat directly below. Mainsails are more complex than jibs. That is to say, mainsails require more and different lines to control their trim than jibs. Sit down in the cockpit and study the mainsheet. Notice that it has several "parts" running up and down between pulleys (called blocks in sailing speak), one set of blocks shackled to the boom, the other to the boat. Because the weight of the wind in the mainsail is too great to handle with a single line, those multiple parts running through blocks afford enough mechanical advantage to overcome the wind force (load) in the sail.

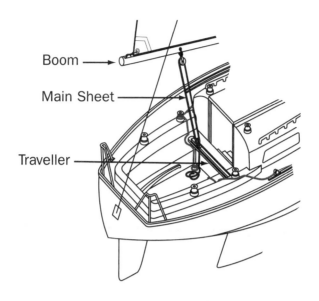

Boom

Main Sheet

Traveller

A typical multi-part mainsheet arrangement showing the block at the boom and that at the deck, including the cam cleat that captures the tail of the sheet. *Illustration © 2009 www.marineillustration.com.*

The lower block on the mainsheet is attached to a movable "car" mounted on a track running side-to-side (athwartships) across the boat. This car and track is the traveler. The traveler's control lines are attached to the lower mainsheet block such that it can be raised—pulled up to windward—or lowered (dropped) to leeward along the track. You'll see a variety of traveler arrangements depending on the size of the mainsail, but they are all rigged to accomplish the same thing: to adjust within limits imposed by the length of traveler track the angle of the mainsail to the wind without changing the tension, the trim, on the mainsheet. Here's the rule of thumb: When sailing to windward in light air, you raise the traveler to bring the boom up along the centerline of the boat. But as the wind pipes up and you have all the power you need, you can dump some of the wind's force by lowering the traveler. You don't change the shape of the main by doing so, but some of the wind's force is allowed to slide past the mainsail. Again, because of its athwartships position, you either "raise" the traveler to windward or "lower" it to leeward.

The position of the traveler—where on the boat it's mounted—will also determine where the mainsheet is positioned, since the mainsheet is always connected to the traveler track. And where the traveler is mounted represents another compromise inherent to sailboat design, an important one, in this case. On cruising boats, the traveler is often mounted on the aft end of the cabin top in order to get this knee-knocking crossbeam out of the cockpit. However, that means that the upper part of the mainsheet must be attached to the middle of the boom, referred to as "mid-boom sheeting." The disadvantage is that a boom sheeted from its midpoint cannot be pulled in close to the centerline of the boat. In other words, the main cannot be as finely trimmed as when the traveler is mounted such that the sheet pulls on the back of the boom: "end-boom sheeting." That requires the traveler to be mounted as far aft as the end of the boom—that is, in the cockpit. But there is another, perhaps more important, disadvantage to cabin-top-mounted travelers. That placement moves the mainsheet—arguably the most impor-tant sail control on the boat—out of the helmsman's reach, especially on bigger boats. You're sailing to windward in a brisk breeze, when a heavy gust blows in, and the boat heels precipitously. If the traveler were in reach of the helmsman, he or she could smartly lower the traveler, spilling wind, and the boat would flatten out. With mid-boom sheeting, quick response on the traveler is not possible unless tended by a dedicated main trimmer, and most cruisers don't sail with a person positioned by the traveler. Still, and not un-reasonably, most cruisers would consider mid-boom sheeting a worthwhile trade-off to get the traveler out of the cockpit to make way for their legs.

The outhaul is another control unique to mainsails. Attached to the clew, it tightens or loosens the foot of the main depending on wind velocity and direction relative to the boat's heading. The tail of the outhaul is typi-cally led forward inside the boom to an exit hole and a cleat mounted near the forward end of the boom. All race boats have adjustable outhauls. On most cruising boats the outhaul is not rigged to allow much fore-and-aft movement. It's merely an attachment point for the clew.

The boom vang, still another mainsail control, is rigged to pull down on the boom. The forward (lower) end of the vang is mounted near the back of the mast at or near the deck, and the aft (upper) end of the vang is shackled to the boom several feet aft of the gooseneck. The vang's purpose is to exert downward pull on the leech.

When the sails are pulled in tight along the centerline, as when sailing to windward, the mainsheet exerts adequate downward pull on the boom and the mainsail. In that case, no vang tension is necessary. But when the wind is blowing over the back of the boat, and the boom is eased accordingly outside the lifelines, the mainsheet, angling outboard horizontally, no longer pulls down on the boom. The force of the wind on the sail therefore tends to cause the boom to rise, and this in turn causes the leech of the main to sag off to leeward, spilling wind. Tightening the vang lowers the boom to a more efficient position roughly parallel to the surface of the water. Keep in the back of your mind for now that the vang, like the sheet, is a leech control. And this suggests a broader principle about sail trim worth noting now to be elaborated upon later: The various lines control individual parts of each sail, luff, leech, and foot. By easing or tightening their respective lines, you change the angle of the sail to the wind or you change the shape of the sail. When you have the parts working together in unison and in balance, you have correctly trimmed your sails.

You have a luff control in the halyard. Halyards hoist sails; that's their primary job. But they have this more subtle function as luff tensioner. By hauling hard on the halyard, you move the draft position (the deepest part of the curve in the sail) forward. Conversely, if you ease the halyard, the draft position moves aft. The Cunningham is an additional, specialized mainsail luff tensioner used only when sailing to windward. (Cunningham takes an initial capital because it was named for its inventor, the famous sailor-adventurer Briggs Cunningham.) It's simply a line fixed to the boom that runs up the main luff a foot or so above the tack through a cringle in the sail and back down to a cleat. I'll have much more to say later about luff and leech controls and why, sometimes, you want a full, round, "back-drafted" sail shape and other times you want flat, streamlined sails with the draft forward. But for now, focus on the names of the controls and the general concept of their purpose.

Finally, let's add two more mainsail controls—the boom topping lift and the jib leech lines—which may be viewed as secondary lines.

The mainsail supports the boom when the sail is set. When it's not, the aft end of the boom is unsupported and, left to its own devices, would drop into the cockpit. That's where the topping lift comes in. The topping lift ("topper" in the slang) runs from the aft end of the boom to the top of the mast. When the main is set, the topping lift unnecessary, the line lies limply along the leech of the main. A fairly recent development, the rigid or hard boom vang, which is a spring-loaded metal tube instead of a line, obviates the need for a topping lift. But always make sure before you lower the main that the aft end of the boom is supported by a topping lift or a rigid vang. (Still a fairly inexperienced sailor, I took my parents for a spin in someone else's boat to demonstrate my new skills. They were suitably impressed until we returned to the mooring, where I doused the mainsail without tightening the topping lift, and the boom dropped on my father's skull.)

Very thin cords are often run within pockets sewn into the leeches of the jib and main. The most important of these is the jib leech line. Like the main, the jib is designed with a degree of curve in the leech. But the jib leech curve is not supported, like the main's leech, by battens. Unsupported, the jib leech tends to flutter when sailing to windward, and this is annoying as well as inefficient. To arrest the flutter, tighten the leech line. If after doing so, the leech "hooks" to windward, then you've overtightened the leech line. Ease off until the leech is flat, but not flapping. (However, the repeated need to tighten the jib leech line might indicate that the leech has been stretched beyond design length, which usually means you need a new jib.)

STABILITY

You see it time and again when a green sailor comes aboard in a brisk breeze. A gust sweeps in and the boat heels sharply. The new sailor's eyes go wide and his knuckles whiten as he clabbers for a handhold, any handhold, in the face of imminent capsize. In choosing to take up sailing, he didn't bargain on capsizing. But the boat doesn't capsize. The gust passes, and the boat comes back up to an even keel. So why didn't it capsize? It felt like it was going to, lying on its side like that, the mast maybe 30 degrees shy of vertical. To answer that good question, we need to look at the unseen parts of the boat below the waterline. But before we do that, let's examine why sailboats heel (tip sideways) in the first place. After all, motorboats don't heel.

The wind, even when it's relatively light, exerts real force on the sails as they translate wind force into motive power. You'll feel that force spread throughout the boat like a bolt of electricity. Touch a jib sheet under load, and it feels more like an iron bar than a rope. It's really quite impressive, the power contained in those pieces of fabric we call sails. The trouble is, the laws of physics dictate that most of the wind's force—when the wind blows from over the front of the boat—wants to push the boat over on its side. Only a relatively small portion of the wind's force devotes itself to moving the boat forward. In the language of boat design, a degree of force is referred to as "moment," and so here we're talking about heeling moment. There's no getting around that law of physics. It can't be challenged; it can only be compensated. So what compensates for the inevitable heeling moment? The answer is that part of the boat you can't see because it's underwater. It's called the keel.

If it's useful, think about sailboat stability in terms of a seesaw. Put a heavy kid on one end, a light kid on the other—the seesaw will be out of balance; it will "capsize" to the heavy kid's side. But put two kids of even weight on the seesaw, and you have balance. The seesaw is stable. In boats, the force (weight) of wind in the sails naturally causes the boat to heel, but it won't, under reasonable conditions, capsize, because this heavy chunk of lead, the keel, mounted on the bottom of the boat counterbalances the heeling moment. You can depend on that, because the boat's designer has mathematically calculated the degree of side forces the sails will generate, and drawn a keel capable of counteracting those forces. In other words, he has designed stability into the boat before it ever leaves the drawing board by supplying in the keel enough righting moment to counteract the heeling moment. This can be further expressed in highly technical language, but let's not. Let's focus on the simple concept—a force in one direction balanced by a force in the other direction. It comes up constantly in sailing.

The key word here is balance, and I'll be talking a lot about that. There is always some technical explanation for balance and for some act the sailor might perform, loosening this or tightening that, to attain balance. But it also has a sensual aspect; you can feel it in the boat and in the sails. It feels good when the boat is balanced. People fall in love with the sport for that feel of balance of forces. You don't often hear sailors talking in the bar about the feel of balance, reverting instead to the technical. Perhaps this is because sailors have folded the feeling into the experience, a kind of given. Or maybe because they think it sounds all squishy and romantic to speak about the harmony between purely natural forces and this wonderful human-made object conceived to make use of natural forces. Most likely it's because sailboat balance is hard to explain—you have to feel it for yourself. Once you have the boat all tuned up in a fresh breeze, at the proper angle of heel, and the boat, the water, and the wind meld into a single unit—then you'll know.

Among the most fundamental manifestations of balance is that relationship between the force in the sails and that in the keel. Dinghies such as Lightnings and Thistles are too small to carry fixed keels. They use centerboards or daggerboards, to supply "lateral resistance" against the wind's force to prevent the boat from skidding sideways. But centerboards and daggerboards are just that: light, small boards. Unlike keels, they are not nearly heavy enough to afford righting moment. So in dinghies, it's up to the crew to supply stability by moving their weight around the boat as needed to counter heeling moment. And this makes dinghy sailing a more athletic activity than keelboat sailing.

But it's not practical or possible to depend on crew weight to counter the press of wind in the sails when the boat gets up around 24 feet and the sail area increases accordingly. At that point you need a significant chunk of lead set low in the water to gain the fulcrum force to oppose the heeling force.

Not so long ago, designers drew long, thin hulls with full keels. In that case, the keel was not an appendage bolted to the bottom, but part of the bottom itself running from bow to stern. The dominant contemporary trend, however, is toward wide-beamed, round-bottomed boats, with fin-shaped lead appendages bolted to the bottom around the midpoint. On fin-keel boats, the rudder is separate from the keel—"detached," in the parlance. Almost no one today is drawing full-keel ("traditional") boats. So in the following discussion, let's concentrate on fin-keel boats, since this is the type you're most likely to encounter. (For the same reason, let's ignore multihulls, catamarans and trimarans, which approach the stability problem in a totally different way. Sadly, multihulls remain rather rare for various reasons, but if the opportunity arises to sail on a cat or tri, seize it by all means.)

A deep fin keel is more efficient than a shallow one. But here the trade-offs begin. Deep keels, while they afford stability, also produce drag—you're literally dragging around a chunk of lead—which naturally slows forward progress. Modern designers seek to minimize drag by drawing thin, blade-like fins. Large, hotshot race boats concerned only with speed take an extreme approach to the problem of stability versus drag by building really long and thin keels, like vertical airplane wings, and then at the very bottom of the keel appending a torpedo-shaped bulb that often weighs more than the hull. The blade-like keel slices cleanly through the water and the heavy bulb down deep affords plenty of righting moment, which in turn allows the boat to carry acres of sail area for speed. However, the resulting draft, that is, the distance between the waterline and the deepest part of the boat, can approach 20 feet on really big boats. This of course isn't practical for the family cruising boat or the club racer. Real-world boats have to decrease draft while still maintaining stability. If, for instance, your home waters are in the Chesapeake Bay or the Florida Keys, you won't be happy with a boat that draws 6 feet. But if you decrease draft by shortening the keel (it's called shoal draft), thereby sacrificing some degree of stability, then you must also decrease sail area when the wind pipes up; otherwise the heeling moment will overcome the righting moment. At the very least, with a shoal draft boat, you will likely lose upwind performance.

FORM STABILITY

One of the most obvious differences between those traditional and modern boats is the width of their beams. (Beam is the side-to-side width of the boat at its widest point.) If appearance is the criterion, the traditional boat wins hands-down. Few nautical craft of any sort are more beautiful in form than a long, thin hull, a Bermuda 40, say, or a Concordia, with those elegant overhangs at the bow and stern. Because they are long and thin, traditional boats are prone to heeling. When a brisk wind blows from over the front of the boat, she'll settle in often at a 20- to 30-degree slant. A modern, wide-beamed boat resists heeling because of the buoyancy afforded by the sides of the boat, specifically by the bilge, that turn of the hull where the topsides meet the waterline. Thus, a degree of stability is designed into the form of the hull, and as a result the designer can decrease the depth of the keel and/or increase the sail area. But there is a trade-off here; in sailing there is always a trade-off, compromise a fact of life. Modern designs must be "sailed flat." If you allow them to heel too much, then that bulging bilge turns into an impediment to progress through the water.

Waterline length is another factor to consider. Modern designs tend to increase waterline length as much as possible, and sometimes the waterline length and the overall length of the boat are equal. This matters because speed is a mathematical function of waterline length. In other words, boats with long waterlines will always be faster than those with shorter waterlines.

But this may be a digression from the important, recurring theme: balance. Sure, some bad boats come out every now and then, but not often. Most boats, you can safely assume, are stable. The designer has designed balance into the boat. Then it remains to the sailor to sustain that balance designed into the boat by properly trimming the sails to fit the wind direction and velocity. The concept of balance is important enough in practical sailing terms to delve into the technical:

The center of effort is the calculated location where the one total force from all the sails is exerted. In a sloop, there is a center of effort in the headsail and another in the mainsail. To calculate these centers of effort, the designer simply draws a line from each corner of the sail to middle of the opposite side; the center of effort is situated at or near the point in the sails where these lines intersect. But the actual center of effort—where the one total force is exerted—is a combination of that in both sails. This location will vary according to the size and shape of the sails, but generally speaking the actual center of effort is situated about halfway up the mainsail slightly aft of the mast.

The center of lateral resistance is the calculated point where the one total hydrodynamic force is exerted on the keel and the rudder. This, too, depends on the shape of the hull, but in a fin-keel boat, the center of lateral resistance is usually situated near the center of the keel.

To attain balance between the two opposing aerodynamic and hydrodynamic forces, the designer draws the hull and sail plan such that the center of effort lies directly, or nearly so, above the center of lateral resistance. To exercise the principle, let's pause to visualize what would happen to balance if, say, the center of effort were situated aft of the center of lateral resistance. The wind force would then press on the back half of the boat, thereby pivoting the bow of the boat into the wind.

To compensate for this situation—called weather helm—the sailor would have to exert constant force on the helm to keep the bow away from the wind. A little weather helm is a good thing, supplying a degree of "feel" to the helm. But too much weather helm means that the rudder must be kept constantly off to one side or the other of the boat's centerline. Not only does this slow the boat due to increased drag, it's annoying. It means the boat is out of balance. Heavy weather helm (or its opposite, lee helm) is rare in today's designs. You're far more likely to encounter boats with neutral helm—no feel. However, the important point for us is that the designer has done his work by drawing a balanced hull and sail plan. Maintaining that balance through a range of conditions is up to the sailor.

FEEL

Throughout this book, I will stress the sensual aspects of sailing, not to sell its appeal but to speed the learning curve. Feel the boat. And what do you feel for? Balance. Sailboats are highly communicative. They will tell you, sometimes without subtlety, when they like how you're handling them and when they don't. If, for instance, a boat suddenly develops weather helm, if the bow insists on turning toward the wind, then the problem likely lies in the trim of your sails. If the boat heels excessively (20 degrees is usually "excessive"), then there is something wrong with your sail trim. And by the way,

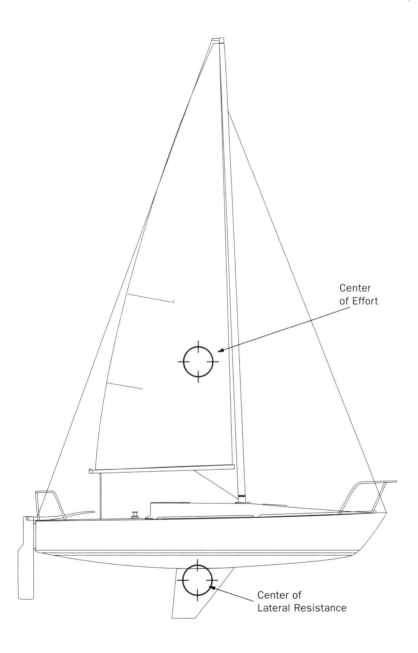

Center
of Effort

Center of
Lateral Resistance

If the center of effort is positioned above or nearly above the center of lateral resistance, the boat will likely feel balanced.

when modern boats heel excessively, they tend to pivot around their keels, and their bow wants to turn into the wind. In that case, bad sail trim (too tight) will induce weather helm. This is an example of heavy-handed communication between boat and sailors. Sailboats communicate more subtly in the language of motion, but if you feel for them, you'll get the messages. They are not mysterious or abstract. So let me suggest right here, and repeat later, that you devote your attention in your early sailing experiences not to the ropes and the hardware but to two questions:

First—always first: Where is the wind?

Second: How does the boat feel?

Soon both will become second nature. You won't even have to ask.

SUMMARY

Please study the language; we'll have to use sailing lingo routinely from now on. But please also consider the following, first, a suggestion as to routine practice and, second, a general sailing principle.

I claimed earlier that all sailboats are generally the same because they employ the same means and methods to derive motive power from the wind. I said also that the sails and the sail-control lines carry the same names. However, there is wide variation boat-to-boat in the position and layout of the running rigging, that collective term for the sail-control lines. So to repeat an earlier suggestion, when you go aboard an unfamiliar boat, walk around the deck identifying all the lines and their layout on deck and at the mast. If you're not sure what's what, ask the owner or an experienced crew. They'll be happy to explain. (By the way, don't try to hide your inexperience by remaining silent; that'll retard your learning process. Ask questions.)

As to the general sailing concept, this might prove a useful way to think about the behavior of a sloop under sail: The sloop carries a mainsail mounted on the mast and boom, and a headsail of varying size attached to the headstay. Both contribute to moving the boat, but in slightly different ways. For now, the important point is how they act to balance the boat, especially when the wind blows from over the front of the boat. The headsail pulls the bow away from the wind. The main wants to lever the bow toward the wind. When both sails are working properly together, the opposing forces align. The boat will be balanced. And you'll know that, because the boat will tell you. There will be little or no pressure on the helm. If you release the helm entirely, the boat will more or less sail herself. She's happy. Trouble is, conditions change. The wind pipes up, or drops; waves get up or diminish. You then have to help her find a new balance by adjusting the trim of the sails. That's what most of the rest of this book is about.

But first let's consider that which moves the boat and determines how we trim sails: the wind.

3

WIND

I N OUR DAY-TO-DAY TERRESTRIAL LIVES, wind is largely irrelevant. Ashore, we notice wind when it climbs to extreme velocities and breaks things or when it remains absent on a hot, muggy late-summer afternoon. In sailing, it's worth repeating, everything begins with and proceeds from wind; wind is the organizing principle behind sailing. So the very first step in learning to trim begins not with the sails and their manipulation but with wind awareness.

The sun causes wind by heating Earth's surface unevenly. Somewhere it is daytime, and the Sun is delivering a hot dose of solar energy to Earth. Somewhere else it is nighttime, and the land quickly cools off. So the Sun heats Earth unevenly on a daily basis. Near the equator, the Sun's energy strikes Earth at near right angles. Moving toward the pole, the incident solar energy grazes Earth at ever-increasing angles, delivering less and less heat with the increase of latitude. The disparity in temperature between the low latitudes and the high is the basic mechanism driving global wind patterns such as the trade winds in the tropics, the prevailing westerlies in the mid-latitudes, and the subpolar easterlies. Where there are disparities in temperature, there are necessarily disparities in pressure. As everyone knows, heat rises, and doing so leaves a sort of vacuum. Nature, disliking disparities in the system, tries to equalize pressure by sending air from regions of high pressure to regions of low pressure. Because Earth rotates, the flow of wind is deflected around the regions of high pressure and low, clockwise and counterclockwise, respectively (in the Northern Hemisphere). With apologies to meteorologists for the simplification, all wind, from afternoon zephyrs at the beach to category-four hurricanes, originates with the "downhill" flow of air from areas of high pressure to areas of low pressure. The result is weather, and when sailors use the word weather, they mean wind.

We identify wind by the direction from which it blows, as for instance an "east wind" or a "south wind," also referred to as an "easterly" or a "southerly." This makes common sense, because it is from that direction the wind will meet your sails no matter which direction you're heading. We could be more specific and name the direction of the wind in degrees of the compass, saying, for an easterly, that the wind is from 90 degrees, and from 180 degrees for the southerly. But in practice, the most common way sailors identify wind is in the form of an angle relative to the centerline of their boat.

The centerline of a boat, its fore-and-aft axis, runs from the point of the bow to the middle of the transom. The direction of the wind always forms some sort of angle relative to the centerline. That angle determines where a sailboat can go and cannot go, it dictates how we should trim our sails, and, in combination with the wind speed, it determines how fast the boat will go. Wind-angle awareness has become instinctive to the experienced sailor. But new sailors, distracted by onboard activity, often lose their bearings as to the wind angle, and confusion inevitably results. Sailing only makes sense when we understand relative wind angles. That's why I encourage the new sailor to ask this question constantly: Where is the wind? Is it blowing over the bow? Over the beam or the stern? And where will it blowing in relation to the centerline if I change course? Indeed, angles are so fundamental to sailing that they all have very old names. And collectively they are called points of sail.

POINTS OF SAIL

Please immerse yourself in this illustration. You might find an object or a model boat to serve as a visual aid, and "turn" it through an imaginary

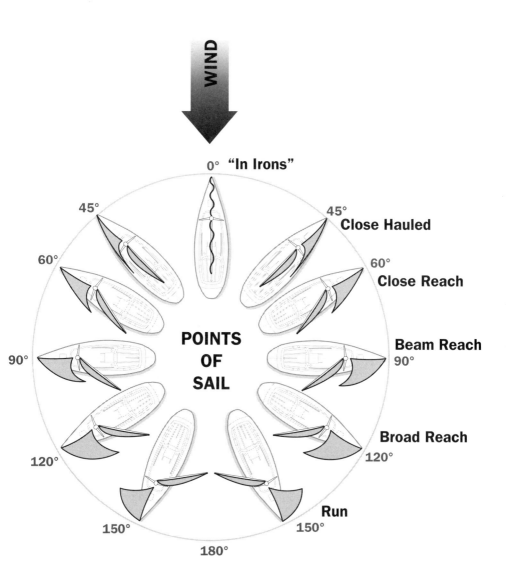

Illustration © 2009 www.marineillustration.com.

wind steady from a single direction. Then perhaps go at it from the opposite perspective—keep the boat's heading stationary and let the wind shift around it. Then take it a step farther by trying to picture where the wind will be if you turn, say, 90 degrees in one direction or another from your "present" heading. It might even be helpful to set up a portable fan to supply "wind," instead of merely imagining it. Whatever your style of learning, focus it at this early stage on understanding points of sail. And think always as you do so in terms of angles—that formed by the centerline of the boat (in other words, what direction your bow is pointing)—and the other limb of the angle, that formed by the wind direction. If the angle changes, either because you turn the boat or because the wind shifts, then you'll need to adjust the sail trim accordingly. But for now, the important step is to grasp the general concept of relative wind angles as illustrated in "points of sail."

WIND WORDS

UPWIND/DOWNWIND

Sailors shorten them to up or down as indication of both direction and boat heading. You'll turn the boat up—toward the wind—or down—away from the wind, which implies of course awareness of the answer to that question, Where's the wind? Say you're sailing with the wind blowing over the starboard side on a beam reach. To "take her up" requires a right-hand, or starboard, turn onto a close reach, and the sails would need to be trimmed (pulled in) to the new point of sail. If you take her farther up onto a beat, you would be sailing on a starboard tack. She won't go up any higher. If you try to press her closer to the wind, she will slow down and the sails will begin to flutter, or luff, like flags. Of course the same principle applies with the wind blowing over the port beam. In that case, to take her up requires a left-hand, or port, turn through a close reach onto a port tack. (A boat is said to be on port tack when the wind is blowing over her port bow, and vice versa.) In some cases, depending where you

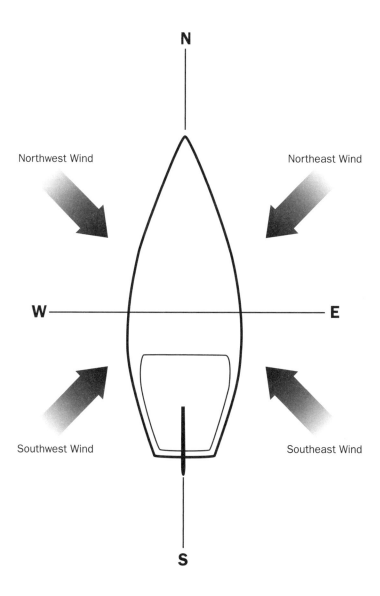

Wind is designated by the direction from which it blows. This makes sense because that is the direction from which wind meets your sails.

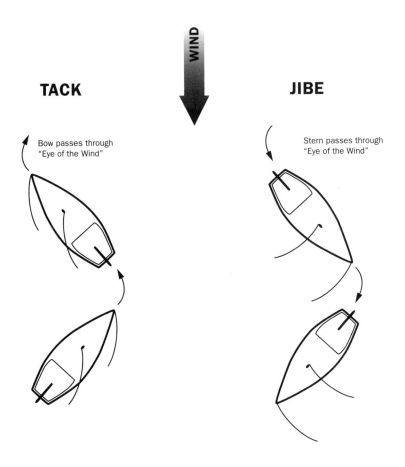

The difference between a tack and a jibe is determined by which part of the boat passes through the eye of the wind.

want to go in relation to where the wind meets the centerline of the boat, you will need to turn either the bow or the stern through the "eye" of the wind, the direction from which the wind blows. Turning the bow through the eye of the wind requires you to tack. Turning the stern through the eye of the wind requires you to jibe. I'll of course have more to say about both maneuvers in a later chapter.

WINDWARD/LEEWARD

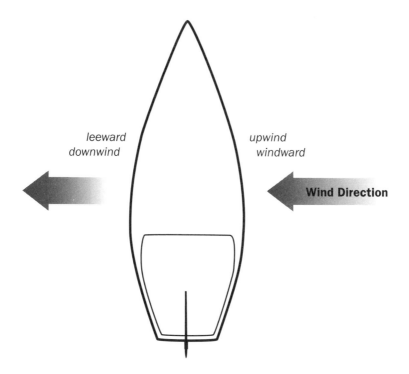

There is a windward (upwind) and leeward (downwind) side to everything, including sails. Direction or position is often designated in these terms. For instance: "The buoy on our leeward bow."

On a boat, there is always a windward side and a downwind or leeward (pronounced LOU-ard) side to everything, including sails. These two words also refer to the direction of things—rocks, buoys, other boats—outside your boat. For instance, you might hear, "The boats to leeward seem to have more wind." Obstructions lying to windward (or to weather) such as rocks, shoals, and anchored boats are less threatening than those lying to leeward, since boats sailing to windward tend to slide sideways or make leeway. However, boats sailing on the downwind side, or in the lee of an island, will ex-

Land lying downwind of you is a lee shore. Beware of this situation. Current and/or leeway can set you sideways into bad water.

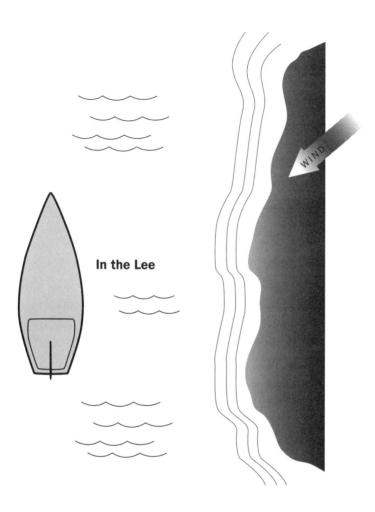

In the Lee

When there is land between you and the wind, you are "in the lee." This is a safer condition than the lee shore, but the wind flow will be disturbed on the leeward side of land.

perience diminished or disturbed wind. This can be a good thing if you're seeking shelter from heavy wind or looking for a quiet anchorage, but it's not so good if you're trying to get past the island in light winds. By the way, wind is sometimes referred to as air, as in for instance light air or heavy air.

"SEEING" WIND

The flow of air we call wind is invisible, yet as a real physical force it affects things like flags, smoke, and leaves, indicating its presence by moving them. You don't need to be an old salt to recognize that. But as sailors, those indicators, while useful, are too general for our specialized needs. We need to observe more subtle aspects of wind.

Let's say you've been invited aboard a friend's boat for a leisurely daysail with a sufficient number of experienced sailors that you have no onboard responsibilities and no pressure to perform. You need only observe and absorb. Let's say further that your friend keeps her boat out on a mooring at a yacht club or marina. You can begin to observe wind before you step aboard, as you walk down the dock toward the launch.

If you're sailing from a yacht club, you will see plenty of flags for a coarse-grained indication of wind direction and velocity. But look a little closer; practice noticing whether the wind is blowing straight off the water onto the flags or whether an object, say the clubhouse, lies between the wind and the flags. (If so, then the flags are said to be in the lee of the building.) When the free flow of wind is disturbed by a vertical object in its path, the flow temporarily changes in both velocity and direction. As wind tries to get over or around the object, it leaves a shadow of windlessness directly on the downwind side of the object. A bit farther downwind the flow is still disturbed, turbulent, until, still farther downwind, the wind regroups into a free flow. I bring this up now as something to notice, because the behavior of wind as it flows around those triangular things we stick up on the mast is fundamental to sailing. Sails work because, unlike buildings, they redirect and accelerate the flow of wind such that they power our boat. Sails are airfoils, and as we'll see, they generate lift on certain points of sail just like an airplane wing.

But that's getting ahead of ourselves. Let's stick to what we can observe out in the mooring field with the aim of viewing the environment through sailors' eyes. Pause at the head of the dock and study the boats in the mooring field. Are they all pointing into the wind? If so, then in nautical lingo, they are said to be lying to the wind. If the boats are pointing every which way, chances are they're lying to a changing tidal current, and the force of the current is stronger than wind's force. That being the case, it means that this won't be a great sailing day. On the other hand, the wind might build as the sun heats up the land. Keep an eye on the moored boats; notice change. If they all begin to swing in the same direction, that could mean either that the breeze has picked up enough to overcome the influence of the tide or that the tide has completed its change, and now all the boats are lying to the tide. But let's assume a moderate breeze is blowing, that it's coming off the water, and that there are no obstructions to its free flow. It's a perfect sailing breeze. Now from the end of the dock, you can employ one of the best wind indicators of all—your face.

Look directly into the breeze and pivot your head until you feel its flow equally on both ears. You're now looking at the true wind direction. If the wind were blowing a few knots faster, you could also use your ears to hear the wind equally on both sides of your head. Sailing is a sensual sport. Never mind the technical stuff for now. Feel the wind.

As you ride the launch out to your friend's boat, notice the little arrows mounted on the mastheads of the moored sailboats. The simple device, a miniature wind vane, is known generically as a Windex after the company that makes it. As long as the boats remain tied to their moorings, the Windex is a totally reliable indicator of wind's actual (true) direction. But now look closer. Are all the arrowheads pegged dead into the wind? Or are they oscillating? Unless a major weather front is coming through, or unless some unusual local phenomenon obtains, the wind will not suddenly change direction in a major way. In other words, a southwest wind will not suddenly shift northeast. However, no wind is steady—even steady wind. It almost always varies in direction and velocity within limits. It oscillates sometimes as much as 20 degrees, and it puffs and lulls. Few landsmen would notice or care, but those small changes matter to sailors. If you notice that the arrows are oscillating a bit, then look still closer. Are the oscillations steady and therefore predictable? Could you time them? Look for a pattern.

Now before actually boarding the boat, let's talk about that other aspect of wind to be considered along with its direction—velocity. A wind's velocity is most often measured in nautical miles per hour or, in proper language, knots (we don't say "knots per hour"). The nautical mile as a unit of distance and speed is firmly based in geography, whereas the statute mile (1.15 nautical miles) and the kilometer (1.85 nautical miles) are arbitrary, agreed-upon units of distance. One degree of latitude the world round contains 60 nautical miles, and one nautical mile equals $\frac{1}{60}$ of a degree, or one minute, of latitude. The knot as a unit of speed is applied both to the wind's velocity and the boat's speed of advance, either through the water or over the bottom (the two aren't always the same).

Most experienced sailors can estimate the wind's velocity within a knot or two by feeling it on their face or by observing familiar visual, environmental references. If the flags stand straight out, if whitecaps kick up on protected waters, then you're likely seeing wind in excess of 20 knots. In the open ocean, you can expect whitecaps at about 12 knots. Twenty knots can be a handful in an 18-foot dinghy. Count on getting wet, and in the gusts you might have to look sharp to keep the mast pointing skyward. (A safety rule in some dinghy races says that if conditions require wet gear, they also require life jackets. When the wind pipes up over 25 knots, many dinghy races will be postponed.) However, in a 35-foot cruising boat, 20 knots will make for brisk, fun sailing. It may have been that kind of day on a friend's boat that induced you to take up sailing in the first place.

Wind force is a blood relative of wind velocity. And there is nothing like sailing to remind you that wind exerts a real force on things stuck up vertically, such as masts, sails, and sailors, in its horizontal flow. The force—the brute power—exerted even by moderate wind, particularly when sailing into it, surprises most new sailors. The laws of physics insist that when the wind velocity doubles, the force of the wind quadruples. A 20-knot wind is not twice as forceful as 10-knot wind; it exerts four times the force. You can't amend the laws of physics, but you are not helpless in the face of rising wind. You can respond first by flattening the sails, and then, if you're still overpowered, by shortening the size of the sails, by reefing. (We'll discuss the techniques of reefing in a later chapter, but for now it's worth remembering the advice of that inventor, yacht designer, and American genius L. Francis Herreshoff: "Reef early and often.")

Now let's observe the wind from aboard your friend's boat on this, a perfect sailing day—flat seas, no current, and a moderate, dependable breeze of 13 or 14 knots. (I used to race Lightnings against a woman who called this a "thinking breeze"—not so strong that she had to struggle to keep the dinghy on an even keel, and not so light and fluky as to be frustrating and seemingly inexplicable.) Watch the experienced crew run the lines and bend on the sails, but remember that you have no onboard responsibilities and no pressure to perform. All you need to do is observe the wind.

While at the mooring, the true wind direction and the boat's head will be the same. The boat's compass indicates the direction the bow is pointing. Therefore, while the boat is lying stationary to the wind, the compass is indicating the true wind direction as well as the boat's "head." There is no sailing angle. If you left the boat tied to the mooring and hoisted the sails, they would flap uselessly over the centerline. The compass indicates the same wind direction you "measured" with your ears back on the dock, but now it puts nautical numbers to the wind direction. (All sailors need to build a working relationship with the compass.) Say the compass reads 90 degrees. This indicates that you cannot in practice sail east at all; you probably can't sail within 45 degrees of east in a straight line.

Once under way, the compass will cease to point toward the true wind, but it will continue to indicate the direction toward which the bow is pointing. That direction forms one limb in this all-important sailing angle. The wind direction forms the other. The angle will change every time you turn the boat even a little bit, but no matter, the compass will always reveal that one limb. And now, because the boat is still tied to the mooring, the compass is identifying the true wind direction. Ninety degrees. Under way, you can check the true wind direction by poking the bow into the eye of the wind— "shooting" the wind—letting the sails flap over the centerline, and reading the compass heading.

Look around for wind signs and signals. Thirteen to 14 knots, our thinking breeze, will seldom kick up whitecaps on protected waters, though local geography and tidal current can defy such generalizations. However, even the lightest breeze will be reflected on the surface. Since summer wind on the Northeast coast and many other places is notoriously light, many of us find ourselves sitting at the mooring after we've rigged the boat for sailing waiting for wind. Some days we wait in vain. This, too, is sailing. You learn patience with the wind or you chuck it in and go golfing. But when it comes, you can watch the wind's arrival and growth like a developing plot in a novel. First zephyrs riffle the shiny surface with "capillary ripples," spotty at first: a dark patch over there under the bridge, another far astern. They gradually fill in until the surface darkens uniformly. This is still no sailing breeze, probably not more than a knot or two, but there is hope that the atmosphere is bestirring itself in response to some disparity in temperature and pressure to enliven sailors' spirits along with their boats. The Windex ceases its aimless orbiting around the masthead and points to windward. At least now there is a windward. Now we feel the new breeze on our faces; maybe we *will* go sailing today.

In Long Island Sound, for instance, if the breeze is northerly, it's likely to die by midmorning. It's a lingering land breeze that resulted from the nighttime cooling of Connecticut while the water in the sound remained relatively warmer. As the Sun heats the land, that disparity will disappear. But if the light breeze is anywhere between westerly and southerly, a sea breeze, then there is hope that it will build to sailable velocity. If a cold front or a warm front is approaching, then that larger-scale weather system will trump local weather conditions. But we can think of frontal conditions as predictable anomalies. In most places during the sailing season, a typical, a sort of default weather pattern will prevail. In most of the Northeast, the Bermuda High determines conditions, and a similar high-pressure mass dominates sailors' lives in Southern California. Because high pressure is associated with light wind or none, we have to depend on the tightly local breeze that results from the uneven heating and cooling between the land and water nearby. But once the heat engine gets cranking, the local breeze can come up quickly.

While seeking wind signs of your own, talk wind with experienced local sailors. Wind is a major topic of conversation in sailing circles, and the locals will be only too glad to inform you of local wind patterns. But be careful of their certainty. Navigating distance-race boats in Long Island Sound and southern New England waters, I heard the experts "suggest" that, "We'll go to the Long Island side during the day and the Connecticut side at night if the wind is light. That always works." No, far from always. Nothing happens in the atmosphere without cause, but nothing always happens. That you depend on the free motive power presented by wind is both the point and the problem of sailing.

So our southwesterly breeze is building. The boat rocks under us at the mooring. Maybe we have 10 knots now. That won't make for exciting sailing, but it's enough to move a dinghy or small keelboat, particularly upwind, though not a 40-foot cruising boat at anything beyond a crawl. The physics are complicated, mathematical, interesting, and unnecessary for sailors, but wind essentially "adheres" to the surface and pulls up waves—or wavelets, since our growing wind is still light. The true wind direction is always perpendicular to the face of the waves or wavelets; if you get confused as to where the wind is, you can always use the waves to reorient yourself. Notice, also, how the Sun glints on the facets of the wavelets. Looking to windward, notice the pattern of the facets—and then look for changes in the pattern. To repeat, no wind is absolutely steady. A puff as small as 1 knot will register as a darker patch on the water. Even if at this point you are unsure of the practical relevance of puffs and lulls, the important point is learn to pay attention to any available environmental signals of the wind's behavior.

And don't ignore the human-made indicators. Other sailboats are particularly useful. What point of sail are they on? Are they heeling or are their masts straight up and down? Is there more wind out in open water beyond the mooring field? Are there "holes" in the wind pattern on the surface, or is it steady as far as you can see? Take another look at the compass. Has the old heading changed? If so, in what direction? (By the way, a clockwise shift in direction is called a veer; a counterclockwise shift, a back.)

In forty-five minutes, the breeze has developed from dead calm to a fine sailing velocity of 14 knots. It sometimes happens that way, to everyone's

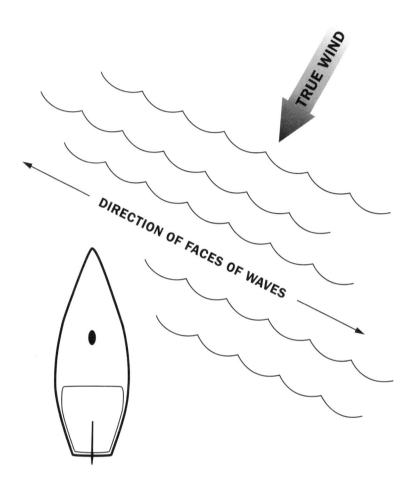

You can use the wave faces to locate the true wind direction.

delight. As the afternoon heat comes on, the wind might increase, so keep in the back of your mind the possibility that it might climb into the 20s by three o'clock. But for a while it will likely remain steady, and it has enough heft to suggest that it will hold.

Your friend, the owner, has a little outboard for her 24-foot keelboat, but she only uses it when absolutely necessary, and this is not one of those times. In this firm breeze, she might as well sail off the mooring under main alone. Later, we'll explain the procedure for doing so and then returning to the mooring without aid from internal combustion.

APPARENT WIND

Apparent wind is the trickster lodged in the physics of sailing. Thus far, speaking of wind, I've modified the word with the adjective *true*. You felt the true wind on your ears; you felt true wind at the mooring. But once you get moving—then the trickster wind, the apparent wind, blows in to confuse the new sailor.

So let's get the boat going. We've set the main at the mooring, sailed out into open water. Now let's set the set jib and put this vessel on a beat sailing into the wind (to windward) . . . What happens then? The wind velocity has increased. By a lot! By maybe 5 knots. Nope, it's just the trickster. The true wind speed has not changed an iota. It's just that we're sailing into it, so we're feeling the speed of the true wind plus the feel of our own forward movement. But since sailing isn't much fun unless the boat moves, and since apparent wind matters—indeed exists—only when our boat is moving, the apparent is the only wind that matters to sailors.

Now let's bear away from the wind. Ease away on the mainsheet, let the jib out, and turn the boat downwind, onto a broad reach or a run. The wind has dropped. Suddenly, precipitously. No. Again, it's the same wind we felt at the mooring. It seems lighter because we're now sailing with it, or, as it were, sailing away from the wind. So we can say generally that the wind we're actually using increases when sailing to windward, and decreases when sailing downwind, while the true wind remains unchanged. This, the difference between true wind and apparent, is as fundamental to sailing as sails.

When I was still green, I found an old salt, a professional rigger, who lived aboard his boat and who expressed a guarded willingness to take me offshore. I wanted to impress him as a fast learner, a natural. One evening

UPWIND

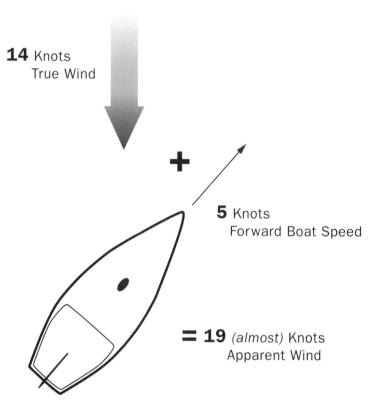

14 Knots
True Wind

+

5 Knots
Forward Boat Speed

= 19 *(almost)* Knots
Apparent Wind

You sail by the apparent wind. The wind the boat (and you) experience increases when sailing to windward.

he abruptly turned the boat from a beat onto a run. Before I could catch myself, I blurted, "Look, the wind has dropped." I noticed his sidelong glance that said, Another hopeless lubber. There are numerous steps in the progression from land person (lubber is too negative, and, besides, I may have been projecting) to sailor. The first is learning the language; the second is understanding the points of sail; third is learning to understand apparent wind.

DOWNWIND

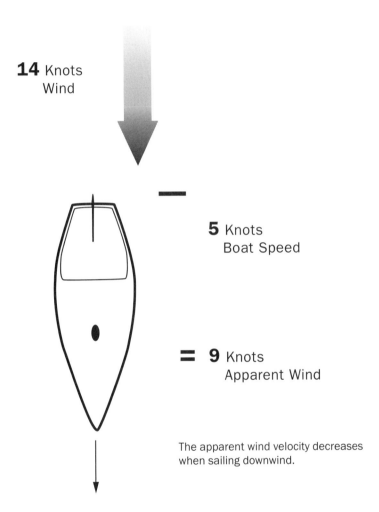

14 Knots
Wind

5 Knots
Boat Speed

= 9 Knots
Apparent Wind

The apparent wind velocity decreases
when sailing downwind.

All things that move create their own wind—an apparent wind. Stick your hand out a car window traveling at 50 miles per hour and you feel a 50 mph wind caused by the car passing through the atmosphere, not by nature. If of course nature's wind were blowing at some velocity and direction, then both the angle and speed of the apparent wind on the car would also change.

Let's begin with that, the simplest manifestation of apparent wind described above, and put some numbers to it:

The wind is blowing 14 knots, and your boat is sailing to windward at 5 knots. Therefore, the mast, the rigging, the sails, and the crew are feeling an apparent wind several knots in excess of 14 knots. If the boat were moving at 5 knots straight into a 14-knot breeze, she would be experiencing 19 knots of wind. But to do that, to move directly into the wind, the boat would have to be motoring. Since she can't sail closer than about 45 degrees to the true wind, the apparent wind velocity would be something greater than 14 but less than 19 knots. To figure the precise apparent wind velocity would require the application of vector arithmetic. The concept, however, is quite graspable without math. And the feel of the boat as she comes alive in the increased apparent wind is one of the sensual pleasures of sailing. She heels a bit, but she feels solid and stable yet streamlined and slippery, a thing bred to pass through the water with optimum efficiency and grace. You can almost see the breeze flowing over the sweet curves of the sails. Everything in balance, nature's forces and human technology in equilibrium, the boat feels happy.

Now let's turn her around and head away from the wind on a dead run. The true wind remains at 14 knots, but you're now moving away from it at 5 knots (these numbers are hypothetical). Therefore, you and your sails are feeling only nine knots. Now she doesn't seem so happy. The boom is as far outboard as the shrouds will allow. The headsail that served us so admirably while going to windward doesn't know what to do with itself, flopping in the wind shadow, in the lee, of the mainsail. You can try pulling it out on the opposite side of the boat from the main, a tactic called wing-and-wing, but there is nothing to support the aft corner (the clew) of the headsail except for the limp breeze. There is a big difference between 18 and 9 knots of apparent wind—a factor of four difference in wind force!—for sailing pleasure.

To exercise the principle, let's up the numbers a bit and say that the true wind is blowing at 20 knots. Now when we tighten up the sails and put her "on the wind" (beating to windward), say we get her up to 6, maybe 7 knots. Now our sails and everything else on the boat are feeling something close to 25 knots of wind. As I said earlier, there is considerably more force in 25-

knots of wind than at 20 knots. Now when you put the boat on a run—and subtract the boat's speed from the true wind velocity—everything quiets down, the stress of wind relaxes, and her motion changes completely, since her sails are now feeling about 15 knots of apparent wind, quite enough to please a light boat, as she sails away from the wind.

Just when you think you have it down—it's really very simple: The apparent increases to windward, decreases downwind—the trickster throws in another variation. That a sailboat moves affects not only the velocity of the apparent wind but also the wind angle. To state the principle before illustrating it: The boat's forward speed also causes the apparent wind angle to decrease. In other words, as boatspeed increases, the apparent wind "moves" forward. Always. Imagine a small powerboat lying stationary in the water with the breeze blowing over her beam, that is, perpendicular to her centerline. (It doesn't matter, in this example, whether the wind blows over her port or starboard beam.) Picture also a flag mounted on the bow of the boat. Responding, as it must, to the true wind, the flag streams downwind also at 90 degrees to the centerline of the stationary boat. Now keep an eye on the flag as the driver adds some throttle and the boat moves forward, thereby making wind of its own. The flag begins to stream aft of the beam. As the boat accelerates, the flag streams still farther aft. When the boat's speed greatly surpasses the wind speed, the flag will stream nearly straight aft along the centerline, responding only to the apparent wind.

Let's put this in the real world by going back aboard the sailboat. The true wind is due north. You want to sail due east, 090 degrees. In other words, the true wind forms a 90-degree angle with the centerline. A beam reach—an excellent point of sail. Point the bow east, ease the main and jib until they flutter at their luffs, then pull them slightly in. You're trimmed up; she accelerates. Have a look at the Windex. You're not sailing on beam reach. The Windex is pointing forward of the beam. You're sailing a close reach. The boat's own velocity has shifted the apparent wind forward. Likewise, if the angle between the true wind and your desired course (your boat's centerline) looks like a close reach, it will become a beat when the boat gets up to speed.

The apparent wind is always forward of the true wind.

**Stationary
Powerboat**

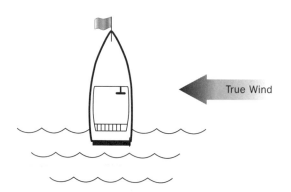

**Forward
Moving
Powerboat**

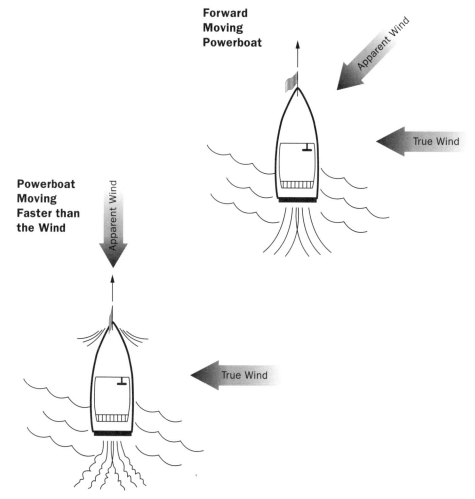

**Powerboat
Moving
Faster than
the Wind**

That dynamic is built into the physics of sailing. Your sails, since they're moving along with the boat, always feel the apparent, not the true wind, and they must be trimmed to the apparent wind. (You'll often hear it referred to simply as the "apparent"; everyone knows what it means.) I'll be talking about and demonstrating time and again these two aspects of apparent wind—velocity and angle—in the following chapters.

THE SEA BREEZE

For those who sail in salt water during the summer months, motive power, most of the time, will come thanks to the sea breeze. I touched on the sea breeze earlier, but because you will become very familiar with its ways and means, we should look a little closer. The sea breeze results from local disparities in temperature between the land and the water. By midafternoon on a bright, hot day, the Sun will have warmed the land, while the water temperature remains relatively cooler—it's in the nature of land to heat up and cool off much more readily than the ocean. In fact, for our purposes, we can say that the sea surface temperature does not change on a daily basis. That's step one in the sea-breeze structure—solar heating of the land.

In step two, the heated land radiates heat upward in the form of a thermal, as hawks and hang gliders well know. This, the vertical component of the structure, creates something akin to a vacuum over the land. In step three, nature seeks to redress the imbalance by drawing in cooler, denser air from the nearest available source—the ocean. This, the horizontal component, is the sea breeze, though in common usage you'll hear sailors refer incorrectly to the sea breeze as the thermal. There will likely be no wind in the morning, because the Sun needs time to sufficiently heat the land. Once this happens, and the thermals surge skyward, they will announce their presence with the formation of puffy cumulous clouds—over land—as the warmed air condenses at altitude. Soon you'll see the breeze begin to riffle the water, and usually, but not always, a sailable breeze will soon fill in.

In San Francisco Bay, they say, you can set your watch to the arrival of the sea breeze, which can honk though the Golden Gate at over 25 knots, and local sailors get a lot of heavy-air experience. On the coast of Maine, the sea breeze blows in cool and moist from the southwest off the Gulf of Maine, producing the famous "smoky sou'westers." Old salts on Long Island Sound contend that the sea breeze is stronger today than when they were young due to all the concrete-and-asphalt development on Long Island, which creates stronger-than-normal thermals. In Buzzards Bay (between Cape Cod and the Massachusetts mainland), the sea breeze comes in relatively harder than elsewhere, because of the funnel shape of the bay and its southerly exposure.

The precise direction of the sea breeze, while largely consistent in each specific place, will depend on the local lay of the land in relation to the ocean. The Long Island coastline, for instance, trends east-to-west with the ocean lying to the south of the island, and so the sea breeze comes in from between south and southwest. Whenever wind blows over or along a coastline, its direction and velocity are influenced by the size and configuration of the obstacles lying it its path. A low, flat coastline will disturb the wind's free flow less dramatically than a high, irregular coastline. When it encounters a steep bluff, for instance, the wind at sea level will bend around the feature, temporarily changing both the wind's velocity and direction, sometimes as much as 90 degrees. This will of course dictate a change in your point of sail. And in proximity to the obstruction, you will likely experience velocity shifts, puffs and lulls, as the breeze tries to re-form itself into a uniform flow. The same thing happens when water in a fast-flowing stream encounters a rock, since water and air, both fluids, behave according to the same physical laws of fluid dynamics.

For our purposes, the point is that the sea breeze in a specific location—your home water—usually fills in from the same direction, and the geography in its path does not change. So with these two givens, you can learn, through observation and on-water experience, how the sea breeze will behave at various spots. While noticing how and when the sea breeze fills in, look for signs on the water and in the environment. Sail over if you can and compare the wind direction and velocity near land with that out in more open water. Chat about it with experienced sailors, but again, beware of the fellow who tells you that such and such always happens when the sea breeze blows; nothing always happens. And that's one of many aspects of the sailor's medium that keeps the sport abidingly interesting.

The sea breeze seldom builds to an unmanageable velocity (recognizing that "manageable" is relative to your experience and the size of your

Position 1

A.M. Sun

Land remains cool.

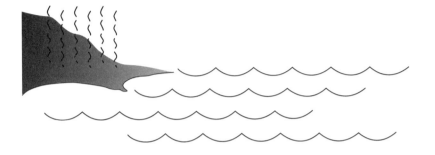

Position 2

P.M. Sun

Thermals

As the land heats up, hot air rises and the sea breeze moves in.

Sea Breeze

boat), because the disparity in temperature and pressure between water and land on a fine summer day is not that great. However, there is another kind of wind—that associated with large-scale weather systems called fronts—that can bring wind best observed from land. With the exception of tropical disturbances, weather in the Northern Hemisphere moves from west to east due to the direction of Earth's rotation and the influence of the jet stream. Masses of anomalously cold and warm air (cold fronts and warm fronts) march across the continental United States in summer and winter, but they are stronger and faster moving in winter. The front is a kind of battle zone between cold and warm, which never meet peaceably in the atmosphere.

Cold fronts are more threatening than warm fronts. When a moving mass of cold—therefore heavy—air encounters warmer air, it wedges the warm air mass rapidly upward where it condenses into ice crystals. As the heavy crystals then fall back toward Earth, they set off an electric charge, and this results in thunderstorms and sometimes dangerously heavy wind.

No sailor should be surprised by the arrival of any front. All you have to do is hear a weather report. Forecasters will shout out the impending front and announce the ETA for your neighborhood. Better still, make it a habit to look at a weather map. If you live in the Northeast and you see on the map a sawtoothed arc stretching from the Great Lakes to the Gulf of Mexico, then you should call off tomorrow's sailing. In the Northern Hemisphere, the wind blows counterclockwise along the face of the front. Tomorrow, when that cold front will have moved east to the coast, the wind will shift (or build quickly) into the south or southwest and come on hard. Wind and rain, thunder and lightning will prevail from Georgia to Maine. If the rain precedes the onset of wind, then the wind will be heavier than if wind precedes rain. The rotten weather will most likely pass quickly; some fronts sprint eastward at 25 knots. When the front passes, the wind will shift clockwise to the northwest, and the day will be clear and crisp. In fact, the northwester is called a clearing breeze, and it will often be stiff. On such days, you'll know that in taking up sailing, you made a good choice.

Admittedly, this is pretty coarse-grained meteorology. But the pattern—southwest winds along the face of the cold front; northwest wind after the front passes—is very common. You've experienced it many times as a landsman, but as such, there was no reason to notice the shift in wind direction or the presence of a repetitive pattern. Again, unless you're sailing offshore, there really is no reason to get caught in the path of a summer cold front, given the ubiquity of weather forecasts and weather maps on the Web, TV, and in newspapers. If you've been lax about checking the forecast or if the front moves into your waters faster than forecasted, you'll still have ample warning of its impending arrival in the form of low, black clouds and towering, dynamic cumulous clouds. If you can't get the boat back to its dock or mooring—sailboats are too slow to outrun foul weather—then duck into the nearest safe harbor and wait it out. And remember, when you're deciding where to wait it out, that the heaviest wind will come from the south or southwest depending on the shape of the front.

* * *

The preceding is only an introduction to the subject of wind. And everything that follows about sail trim and boat handling originates with and proceeds from wind. Thus it's worth repeating several principles:

Where is the wind in relation to your desired course? Where will it be if you change course? Wind awareness is key to the learning process.

Learn to look for wind signals in the environment, both natural and human-made.

Think in terms of angles. The boat's centerline is one limb of the sailing angle; the apparent wind forms the other. The size of that angle in degrees determines how you trim your sails. Study that points-of-sail diagram, since it puts names to the various angles between the centerline and the apparent wind direction.

Remember that crucial distinction between true wind and apparent wind. Once your boat begins to move, only apparent wind matters. The velocity and force of the apparent increase when you sail to windward and decrease when you sail downwind. And because your boat, when moving, creates its own wind, the apparent wind angle always moves forward of the true wind angle. This is a tricky concept to grasp on paper, but far clearer once you actually get on a sailboat. Remember that sailors love to talk about wind; so don't hesitate when sailing with experienced people to ask questions.

Don't let the esoteric language, the lines, and all the bits of hardware distract you at the early learning stages from those basic wind questions (where is it now; where will it be if the boat turns?). Focusing first and foremost on wind awareness will greatly accelerate your learning process.

RIGHT-OF-WAY

Ages ago, some authoritative body decided arbitrarily that when boats are sailing in close proximity, the one on starboard tack has right-of-way. The boat on port tack, said to be burdened, must keep clear. But what if a boat sailing downwind on a broad reach with the wind blowing over the starboard side of her transom (her starboard "quarter," as it's called) encounters a boat on starboard tack? Who has right-of-way when both boat boats are "on starboard"? Someone decided that the leeward boat (farther downwind) has right-of-way, and the boat closer to the wind is burdened. The boat with rights in her favor (either by being on starboard tack or by being the leeward boat) is formally designated the "standon" vessel.

Opposite Tacks

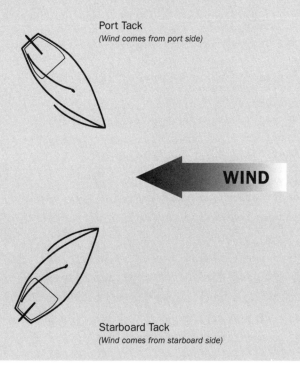

Port Tack
(Wind comes from port side)

WIND

Starboard Tack
(Wind comes from starboard side)

The boat on starboard tack has right of way, and the port tacker must get out of the way.

Same Tacks

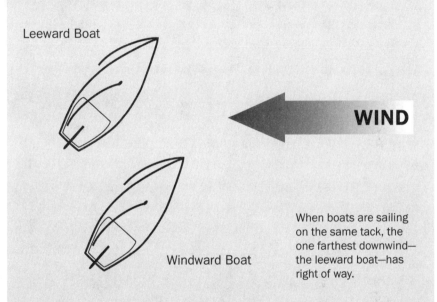

Leeward Boat

WIND

Windward Boat

When boats are sailing on the same tack, the one farthest downwind—the leeward boat—has right of way.

Crossing situations come up all the time on the racecourse, where it often makes tactical sense to aggressively claim your rights, forcing the burdened boat to get out of the way. This is not so when daysailing or cruising. The rules still obtain, but they should be applied according to common sense. Suppose you're out for a leisurely daysail or practice session in an 18-foot dinghy sailing on starboard tack. You see a crossing situation developing with a 50-footer sailing hard on port tack with most of her crew lined up on the windward rail. Do you really want to make this guy tack away? He'll do it, but he won't appreciate your lack of courtesy and good seamanship. You can tack away (or otherwise avoid him) with much less hassle than he can; you might as well give him right-of-way. Wave him across your course while there is still plenty of room between the boats. If you wait too long, you can cause a collision by not claiming your rights if both of you bear away from the wind at the same time. Or you can signal that you're relinquishing your rights by bearing away or tacking while there is still plenty of separation between the boats.

Let's reverse the situation to say that you are the burdened boat because you're either on port tack or the windward boat. Because you're paying attention to your surroundings, you see a starboard tacker sailing toward you. How can you tell whether or not you're on a collision course? With practice and close attention, you'll be able to judge relative speed just by looking, but it takes time to do so reliably. However, you don't have to flee from everybody on the water until you gain enough experience to "eyeball" a crossing situation. There is a reliable visual gauge to help you determine whether or not you're on a collision course.

Look across the mast of the oncoming boat, assuming it's a sailboat, to some land feature beyond. If that point of land is not "moving" in relation to the other boat, then you're on a collision course. You will need to take some action to avoid it. If on the other hand the boat is "making trees on you," in the parlance, then if you hold your course, you will pass either safely behind or ahead of the oncoming boat. When cruising, courtesy and common sense should determine whether and when to claim your rights. When racing, the rules and tactical concerns determine your decision.

Crossing Situations with Powerboats. The old "conflict" between "stink pots" and "rag boats" is boring and stupid. There are plenty of powerboat operators as equally skilled in their game as good sailors in their "blow boats." Without feeling superior, however, remember that it is a lot easier to operate a powerboat than a sailboat in terms of required knowledge and level of attention. This requires us to assume, for safety's sake, that the powerboat operator may be a little short of knowledge and attention. The rules of the road say that a powerboat must, in most but not all instances, give way to a boat under sail. No-tice the phrasing, a boat under sail; if the sailboat is motoring, then under the rules, it's a powerboat. If you're motoring and you encoun-ter the possibility of collision with another powerboat approaching from your starboard side, then that boat has right-of-way. You are burdened. Conversely, if another powerboat approaches from your port side, then you have right-of-way. In another permutation, if you are overtaking another vessel, power or sail, then you are burdened and must keep clear.

Usually crossing situations between powerboats and sailboats re-solve very quickly due to the huge speed differential. But don't ever blithely assume that the powerboater will grant you your rights if you try to cross his bow; don't even assume he sees you. This is not meant to be disrespectful to powerboaters; it's only to say that a collision with one will ruin your sailing day. And don't waste any emotional energy in anger if he blows past you imperviously leaving a wake like an ocean wave. Protect yourself with constant vigilance, and make no assump-tions about what he will or will not do, no matter what kind of boat it is. Keep in mind the old verse:

> Here lies the body of Michael O'Day
> Who died maintaining the right-of-way;
> He was right, dead right, as he sailed along,
> But he's just as dead as if he'd been wrong.

And finally never, ever press your rights over commercial vessels. I'll never forget when in a big regatta on Long Island Sound, an over-zealous race boat skipper cut the bow of a tug pulling a barge, forcing the tug captain to slam on the brakes. The outraged captain called the Coast Guard, which arrived in two boats and threw us all off the sound for one man's stupidity and abject lack of seamanship.

4

LOOKING AT SAILS

S O WHAT DO YOU LOOK FOR WHEN looking at sails? Start with curves. You don't need experience to appreciate the curve in a good main and jib. Just use your aesthetic eye. Sailing is supposed to be aesthetically pleasing. Forget the technical and look at the sails as shapes. Curves, to be pleasing, need to be fair, without bulges or flat spots; they shouldn't be too deep or too flat; they should stream, suggesting motion, flight. For the best view, sit up on the windward rail when the boat is sailing in a straight line with the apparent wind forward of the beam, and look up at the curves formed by both sails. Try to notice the relationship between the curve of the main and that of the headsail. If they're well trimmed, the set of the main and headsail will suggest an interaction, a unity of form. You don't have to be an old salt or a sculptor to see the aerodynamic relationship between the two sails. If a sail looks good, chances are it is good. But this purely visual aspect, like wind awareness, often gets overlooked in the welter of detail and technical blah-blah during the early stages of the learning-to-sail process. Don't let that happen; trust your eye.

This is not to say that you can learn to sail by looking. And of course your eye for a pleasing, fair curve can't teach you how to attain that shape in a sail. But should you find yourself sailing to windward in a fine breeze aboard a friend's boat, you can learn a lot about the objective of sail trim by simply looking up. Looking up is intrinsic to sailing. The trimmers and the driver seem to be paying attention, not chatting or steering with a sandwich in one hand. They're driving the boat fast and well, "in the groove" just for the hell of it, just because it feels good to sail that way. Lean back against the lifelines, tune in to the boat's pleasure, and look at the sails as shapes interacting with "invisible" wind.

Going to windward in a fine breeze, the sails are behaving just like an airplane wing stood vertically. An airplane flies because its wings generate lift when the airflow is induced, by the shape of the curve, to flow over both sides of wing at different velocities. Lift results as the air, flowing faster over one side of the airfoil than the other, creates lower pressure over the surface with the faster flow (the top of the wing, the leeward side of the sail) and the airfoil wants to rise in the case of an airplane wing, or go forward in the case of a sail. Passengers would be alarmed to look out the window at a lumpy, ragged airplane wing. Likewise, you don't want to see lumpy, creased sails. You want fair, smooth curves to induce the air to flow smoothly over both sides of the sail. If it does so without interruption, the airflow will literally pull the boat to windward. Does it look like the air is flowing smoothly over both the windward and leeward sides of both sails?

To observe the vertical curves in the sails, step aft, perhaps behind the helmsman, and look at the leeches of both sails. If the sailors have presented the sails to the wind at the most efficient angle and degree of tension, the leech curve on the jib will be almost parallel to that in main leech. The windward side of the jib and the leeward side of the main are interacting aerodynamically as the jib directs airflow onto the back of the main, accelerating the wind as it does so. Let the shapes wash over you. It's no coincidence that fair, visually pleasing curves are also fast and efficient. Now let's look a bit more technically at the horizontal curves in both sails, best observed from back up on the windward rail, as we edge toward the question: How do we attain those sweet curves?

Most but not all sails come equipped from the sailmaker with horizontal stripes of red or blue material running from the luff to the leech of the main about two-thirds of the way up from the boom and at about the same height on the jib. This is the speed or draft stripe, and it's there as a visual aid to reveal the horizontal shapes, specifically the location of the draft in each sail. Draft is the deepest part of the sail, or, we might say, the amount and location of the greatest curvature. If you've sat near the wing on a jetliner, you've heard a whirring sound during landing approach. That's the sound of the wing flaps on the leading edges being deployed downward. By adding flaps, the pilot is changing the shape of his wings—and thus the airflow over them—in order to maintain lift at slower landing speed. The sailor does the same thing to maintain lift through a variety of wind velocities—by moving the draft position forward or aft.

Sailing to windward in our fine 14-knot breeze, we want relatively flat sails with the draft in the main positioned about halfway between luff and leech, and about one-third of the way aft of the luff in the jib. In this case, the sails are said to be "powered up." One reason why the draft position is located farther forward in the jib than in the main in this powered-up configuration is that the jib is operating at the front of the boat in undisturbed air, while the airflow in the main is disturbed to some extent by the mast. Another reason has to do with the way an overlapping headsail directs air across the leeward side of the main. Here's the rule of thumb: In a fine breeze, like our hypothetical 14 knots apparent, you want the draft forward on both sails when sailing to windward, but in light air, you want to position the drafts farther aft in order for the wind to "adhere" more readily to the sail.

Draft position, as I'll discuss later, is a function of luff tension, which is controlled by the halyards (additionally, by the Cunningham in the main). If you tighten the halyards, the draft visibly moves forward; if you ease the halyards, the draft positions move aft. In this and all cases when I speak about easing/tightening halyards and other lines, I'm talking about relatively small adjustments—they should always be made while looking at the results in the sail, not at the line you're easing or tightening. And here again, the smaller the boat, the smaller the adjustment needed to affect the change in draft position. On a good dinghy, for instance, an ease of 2 inches, or less, is all that's required to move the draft aft, and vice versa. Most sailors, once they've found optimum draft positions for various wind velocities, mark their halyards with Magic Markers or paint and hoist to the appropriate point, given the conditions that obtain at the time. That halyards tend to stretch over time explains why high-tech, no-stretch ropes have found an avid market, particularly among racing sailors.

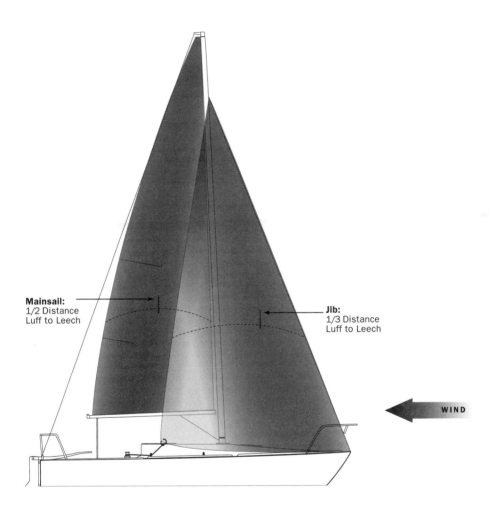

Mainsail:
1/2 Distance
Luff to Leech

Jib:
1/3 Distance
Luff to Leech

WIND

When the boat is sailing to windward at full speed, the draft in jib should be located about one-third of the distance from the luff. In the main, the draft should be located about half way aft from the luff.

THE TELLTALES

Speed stripes as visual aids indicate a semi-stationary shape, that is to say, the draft position will remain unchanged, barring halyard "creep," until you intentionally change it. The telltales, another and perhaps the most important visual aid, reveal the dynamic flow of air around the sails that obtain from moment to moment. Simple pieces of yarn or plastic strips attached to the sails, telltales are about as low-tech as you can get, but they are also nearly infallible indicators of proper trim. Broadly speaking, when the telltales are streaming aft in unison, then the sails are properly trimmed. I've heard sailors say something to the effect, "I don't use the telltales; I sail better by feel." Nope. Not possible. These same sailors tend to overtrim their sails because flat, tight sails tend to feel and look faster than loosely trimmed sails. Those simple strips of yarn feel the wind far more accurately than any sailor.

Notice the placement of the telltales. Several sets of telltales are positioned along and just aft of the jib luff on both sides of the sail. Sometimes owners choose to place green tales on the starboard-tack side of the jib and red on the port-tack side On the mainsail, several single telltales are attached along the leech. While this is the basic pattern—the sailmaker delivers sails with these tales in place—sailors often add more, another set, for instance, running up the jib about one-third of the way aft from the luff and others on the surfaces of the main.

Let's look first at the jib. You're sailing on the wind, sitting on the windward side of the boat watching the tales on the jib luff. One set of tales, usually halfway up the luff, is mounted in a transparent window so that you can see the windward and leeward tales simultaneously. Sailing to windward, the windward and leeward tales are streaming together. But then something changes, and the telltales on the windward side (the inboard side) of the jib begin to flutter and sag. This indicates that the breeze is no longer flowing evenly over both sides of the luff. But why? Probably because the helmsman is trying to steer the boat to high, "pinching," in the parlance. Or it could be that the wind has shifted toward the bow, and the helmsman has neglected to steer down in response. In either case, what in effect is happening is that the tales on the windward side are suffocating in the lee of luff. The tales on

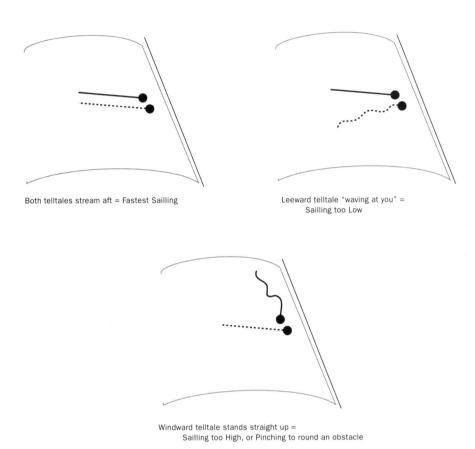

Both telltales stream aft = Fastest Sailing

Leeward telltale "waving at you" =
Sailing too Low

Windward telltale stands straight up =
Sailing too High, or Pinching to round an obstacle

the leeward side will be streaming merrily. The boat slows down. The airflow in the jib has "separated," as they say, because the boat is sailing too high. You can feel as well as see it.

In the opposite case—the windward telltale streaming, the leeward tale hanging—the boat is sailing too low. The air is flowing over the inside, the windward side of the jib, but not over the downwind, leeward side of the jib. When the wind separates from the leeward side of the sail, it devolves into turbulence. Since the motive force is related, as I said when talking about lift, to the airspeed difference between the up- and downwind sides of the sails, the boat slows down. The foil is stalled. (Generalizing, you could say that the aim of sail trim is to keep the airflow smooth, constantly attached, and to avoid creating turbulence.) To reattach the airflow, the helmsman must steer back up, or the jib trimmer can ease the jib until the tales stream aft together.

Now the mainsail telltales. There are usually four attached to the leech, often at the batten pockets. When they all stream straight aft, they are telling you that the back part of the main is serving you efficiently. If the tales are flopping over to the windward side, then the main is trimmed too tight. It's "choked," in the parlance. Ease the mainsheet, and the leech, specifically the roach, will open, and the telltales will stream again. (To repeat: Except when executing a big course change, make your small adjustments and wait to see how the boat reacts.) Most new sailors tend to oversheet, to choke their sails. Ease them as a matter of habit until their luffs flutter, and then sheet them in just enough that the flutter ceases. And, as always, feel the boat as you do so. If you feel slow, sluggish, the first thing to do is ease the sails.

"FLAT" OR "FAT"

These are merely descriptive terms, by no means absolutes. No sail is literally flat, since, as I said, the sailmaker builds curves into every sail. And an old, blown-out, therefore untrimmable sail could be described as fat. But the point is that you can control, according to wind conditions, the amount of curve in your sails. Here's the rule of thumb: When the wind is strong, flatten your sails. When the wind is light, fatten them. Now let's look at the sense behind the rule. "Strong" wind is a relative term directly related to the size of your boat. Let's define strong, then, as enough wind to cause excessive heel, or in different words more wind than you need to drive the boat at her maximum speed. At some point as the wind increases, you will have to reef. But for now, let's address that point, no matter the boat, between too much heel and the need to reef.

You want to spill some wind from your sails; you want to make them less efficient. Start by tightening everything. Tighten the luffs, by hauling on the halyards enough to remove all horizontal wrinkles. If vertical wrinkles appear near the luff, then you've overtightened. Ease off until they go away.

As always, watch the sail as you make the adjustments. When you tighten the luffs, you move the draft, the deepest part of the curves, forward. Tighten the outhaul to flatten the lower part of the main.

Your boat is sailing fast to windward, but she feels skittish; she's heeling too far in the gusts; you have to muscle the helm to keep her bow away from the wind. It's not too bad yet; you're not completely overpowered, but the lee rail is nearing the water. Now is the time to spill some air. If tightening both halyards ("blading" the sails) doesn't spill enough wind to flatten the boat, then you can take additional measures to straighten her up. But take each step one at a time, and wait to observe the results.

Try moving the jib lead aft. This decreases the downward pull on the jib leech, allowing it sag off to leeward, thus spilling air. The result is called twist. You've twisted the sail. You can also twist the main to the same effect by pulling the traveler up to the centerline of the boat and then easing the mainsheet. The upper part of the leech, twisted, will then spill air. If the wind continues to increase, drop the traveler all the way to leeward. Then in the gusts, you can ease some mainsheet, and that will "feather" the main, allowing the wind to slip past both sides of the sail without adhering completely. In the extreme case, you'll be sailing off the jib alone. You will likely feel immediate results by easing the traveler and feathering the main in the gusts. The boat will stand up straighter—and her speed will increase. Remember, the problem isn't that you're going too fast (speed is good), it's that you're heeling too much. Dropping the traveler does not significantly change the trim of the main, only its angular relation to the wind, but dropping the traveler spills wind from the main. In the lulls, take back some tension on the sheet and/or raise the traveler, but stand ready to ease again. This will require a bit of practice to get the timing down, and it is contingent on feeling the boat heel and responding immediately by easing the sheet. If you wait to ease away until the boat heels at an extreme angle, you've waited too long. Remember, when a modern, wide-beamed boat heels, not only does she slow down significantly, but she slides sideways through the water.

On fractionally rigged boats, you can also flatten the main by tightening the backstay. Some new sailors find this counterintuitive. "If you tighten the backstay such that it bends the mast aft, won't that make the sail fuller?" No, when the mast bends, the bow in the middle of the mast pulls cloth for-

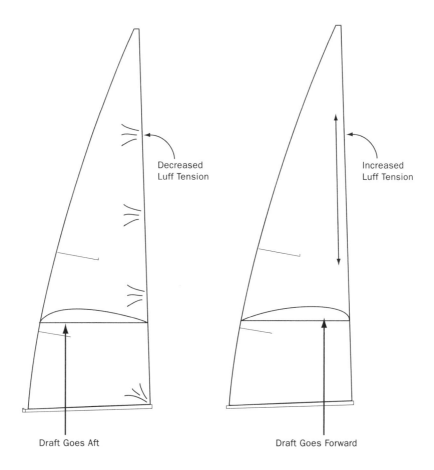

Decreased Luff Tension

Increased Luff Tension

Draft Goes Aft

Draft Goes Forward

Tighten the halyard to increase luff tension in the main. Increased luff tension moves the draft forward, as when sailing to windward. Easing the halyard, until horizontal wrinkles appear at the luff, moves the draft aft, desirable in light air or when sailing downwind.

ward, thus flattening the main. On masthead rigs, tightening the backstay won't bend the mast to nearly the extent as a fractional rig, but it will tighten the headstay, countering its natural tendency to bow under the force of wind in the jib.

If none of these tactics works or if the wind continues to build, then you'll have to take more aggressive steps. You'll need to decrease the size of the jib and/or the size of the main. In other words, you'll have to reef, which we'll discuss in chapter 6.

Turning to the opposite situation, when the wind is light, you want full sails. To feel, as well as understand, why this is true, try an experiment. On a light-air sailing day, light being as always a relative term, tighten everything, luffs and leeches, and drop the traveler to leeward. Feel her struggle as she tries to maintain speed. Your sails are "choked." The light wind can't get a grip on them; it just flows past the sails. The boat will slow in protest. Ease off on the halyards; let a few short, horizontal wrinkles appear in the luffs. Pull the traveler up to windward to bring the boom up to the centerline. Ease the sheets. Remove any backstay tension. Ease the outhaul. Soft sails don't look fast, and in a sense they aren't. But they are efficient; they draw in light air.

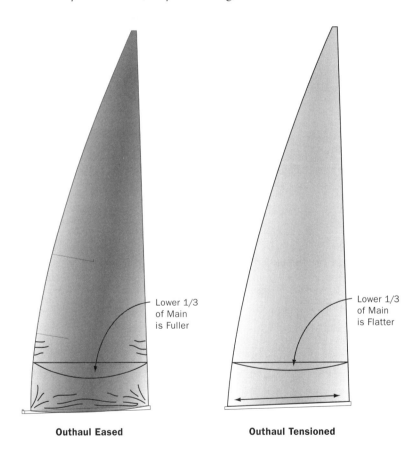

Outhaul Eased   **Outhaul Tensioned**

The outhaul has a similar effect on the lower part of the main as the halyard on the luff. Easing the outhaul makes the lower part of the sail fuller. Tightening the outhaul flattens the lower part of the main.

I've been talking here about "flat" or "fat" when sailing to windward, or at least with the wind blows from forward of the beam. Now let's turn away from the wind and look at the principle from a run or very broad reach, say, with the wind on the stern quarter—the aft "corner" of the boat where the sides meet the transom. It's still a matter of wind velocity, but instead of nature's wind changing, your own apparent wind changes with the new point of sail. Sailing downwind, you want full sails because the apparent has lightened.

Many new sailors seek to avoid all the seemingly confusing variables by setting the sails one way, sort of medium, and leaving them like that. Besides, some boats, due to thickness of their mast and small sail plans, won't respond to fine-tuning anyway—and that's another reason why you should try at the early learning stages to sail small, nimble boats. There are lots of ways to go sailing, and the idea is to enjoy the activity, not to adhere to some notion of the best way to sail. But as a new student of the game, you will profit from recognizing that sails can be shaped in response to different wind conditions, that they can be fattened or flattened, that the draft position can be moved forward or aft simply by tightening or loosening the sail controls. Don't believe it if someone tells you that only neurotic racing sailors concern themselves with that kind of thing, that it doesn't matter, anyway; want another sandwich? That person is expressing a preference, if not a prejudice, as to how he wants to sail, not a truth about sailing itself.

Some of us derive real pleasure from technical sailing, which is to say trimming and steering such that the boat sails at maximum speed and efficiency at least most of the time. Speaking strictly for myself, I can't stand sailing on an indifferently trimmed boat; it feels like an itch I can't scratch. For instance, you'll see boats sail by with their genoa leeches fluttering audibly. The sailors don't seem to care that their jib leech sounds like a playing card in a kid's bicycle spokes, or they don't know that they could stifle the fluttering simply by tightening the leech line. It's ugly, that fluttering genoa leech, that fat, wrinkled mainsail. There is a unique aesthetic component to sailing, and one reason to concern yourself with fine sail trim, which includes sail shape, is that well-trimmed sails look and feel good. Poorly trimmed sails do not. But then, sailing is pretty democratic; there are lots of ways to express yourself, and you can take your choice.

SPEED UNDER SAIL

I was driving marine photographer Billy Black's chase boat one glowering December day about a decade ago. Black was out to shoot the start of a transatlantic speed record attempt by the catamaran PlayStation then owned by the late Steve Fossett. The big, brutal cat was flying for the start mark, Ambrose Light Tower seaward of New York City, and Black, who wanted to get ahead of her for a shot across her bows, motioned me to put the throttles to the stops. His twin outboards roared, leaving a rooster-tail wakes, and at full speed we were doing 28.8 knots according to the GPS. But we couldn't catch PlayStation. She crossed the Atlantic from Ambrose to the English Channel in four days, seventeen hours, twenty-eight minutes. In 2009, another huge French catamaran named for its sponsor, Banque Populaire, covered an astonishing 909 nautical miles in a single twenty-four-hour period for an average speed of about 38 knots! Now even a few monohull race boats are ticking off speeds of 30-plus knots. Needless to say, these are not safe, comfortable boats, but they have revolutionized the very concept of speed under sail.

Sadly, however, few of us recreational sailors will ever get to experience the sensation (and the fear) of 30 knots. I navigated the 80-foot Russian monohull Fazisi in 200-mile race when she reached 15 knots. I'll never forget it, but I haven't come close to that speed in the fifteen years since. During the summer in most active sailing areas, you'll seldom exceed 7 knots. You'll probably see 10 knots if you race on one of today's light, high-powered boats, but few cruising boats ever go that fast. Thirteen knots is beyond the experience of most recreational sailors.

So what difference does it make if one boat is faster by a few knots than another, especially if it isn't a race boat? For one thing, the feel of speed and wild power as a sailboat drives through its very dense medium in a stiff wind is not reflected in those low knot numbers. (Maybe it was fast ride on a well-sailed boat that moved you to take up sailing in the first place.) But in this there is also a fundamental principle of sailing.

In good conditions (obviously not in heavy weather), sailboats should always be sailed at maximum speed. If you're sailing short of maximum speed for a given wind velocity, then something is out of trim, out of balance. If everything is in balance, if she's going at maximum speed, the boat will express her pleasure in plain terms. There will be no argument from the helm; the boat will go in a straight line. You don't have to be an old salt to understand her signals of approval.

5

STRAIGHT-LINE SAILING

L ET'S GET BACK UNDER WAY AND LOOK more closely at the trimming procedures on the various points of sail. Since we're limiting this trip to a straight line—we're not going to tack or jibe— the wind will remain on one side of the boat. But what kind of boat should we "use"?

A generation or so ago, centerboard dinghy sailing was enormously popular. Every yacht club from the Atlantic to the Pacific and every lake in between had fleets of Lightnings, Thistles, and similar one-design race boats (one-design means that all the boats are the same). But today the trend has shifted away from centerboard dinghies, though this is not to say that have vanished; far from it. I learned more about pure sailing in three seasons of hard racing aboard a Lightning than in a decade of big-boat racing. I was amazed at the degree of sail sophistication evident in these little boats. A 2-inch change of setting on this line or that produced immediate, palpable results. If you have a choice of what sort of boat you learn on, by all means choose a dinghy.

However, designed as race boats, centerboard dinghies are tippy, uncomfortable, and overpowered (big sails), characteristics not conducive to a relaxing daysail. They require a degree of athleticism, particularly when the wind pipes up, and as their owners aged and their knees grew iffy, they moved away from dinghy racing. The younger generation did not pick it up in equivalent numbers.

Then in the late 1960s, there arose an entirely new concept in sailboat manufacturing and with it a new kind of boat—the fiberglass, mass-produced, or production sailboat. Before then, if you wanted a 40-foot boat you had to have it designed and built from scratch, and if you had to ask the price—you know. Builders such as Tartan, C&C, Columbia, Cal, and soon J/Boats turned out good boats made of this new stuff called fiberglass with the same mass-production methods Ford used to make cars, and with the same commensurate cost savings. The middle class took up sailing. And what were they sailing? This brand-new idea of a sailboat, a fin-keel sloop with a fiberglass hull impervious to rot, a decent sail plan on an aluminum mast, and it had a cabin below with berths, galley, and, imagine, a head. You could take the family on a weekend cruise, and if you wanted, you could race it against the growing number of similar boats. The cruiser-racer was born. The trend has developed, matured, attracting by sheer market power the best designers. Today, small fin-keel sloops dominate almost every mooring field in the country. All this is to say that, unless you actively search out the havens of dinghy racing, you will likely gain your early experience aboard a fin-keel, sloop-rigged cruiser-racer.

So let's use that as our hypothetical boat, and on the assumption that smaller boats are more educationally productive, let's keep it in the 25-foot range, nimble, quick, with generous sail area, a communicative boat. And let's say that there are three people aboard, a helmsperson—you—and two crew.

BEFORE YOU DROP THE MOORING

Stow your gear and sandwiches below, bearing in mind that this boat is going to heel. If you just drop your stuff on the seat, it will end up on the floor (the "sole," in nautical language). Then take a stroll around the deck. Suggesting liveliness, she'll tip slightly when you step on the side decks. A 40-footer would not move under your weight.

How are the halyards led? The jib is small enough to be hoisted and tightened by hand, no winch necessary, so the tail of the jib halyard will likely be cleated on the mast. Because the mainsail is bigger and because there is some friction to overcome as the luff slides in the mast groove, the main halyard will likely require a winch to complete the hoist. Most likely, the main halyard will be led aft along the deck to a small cabin-top-mounted winch. But there may be variations on this halyard layout. Look around. Where is the boom-vang line led? The outhaul? "Learn the ropes."

Notice the two jib-sheet winches mounted near the cockpit. Winches need (detachable) handles. Stow the handles within easy reach, but not in the winches. Note: Lines are always wound clockwise around winches.

"BEND" ON THE SAILS

In general, when bending on the sails and affixing their running rigging, try always to visualize the sails and their lines when the sails are up and drawing.

The jib might be preset on a roller furler on the headstay, or it might be fixed to the headstay with "hanks," spring-loaded clips permanently attached to the jib luff. In the latter case, bring the sail up from below, attach the tack to the deck-mounted shackle at the foot of the headstay, and then clip on the hanks, making sure they all go onto the headstay in the same direction. Next attach the halyard shackle to the head of the sail, making certain that the halyard runs freely from its exit at or near the top of the mast—that, for instance, it isn't wrapped around the headstay. Now tie the jib sheets to the clew using bowlines. (If you learn no other knot, learn to tie a bowline. You may find bowline tying a frustrating learning process at first, but keep working at it. Suddenly you'll get it, and you'll be able to tie a bowline with your eyes closed.) Run the jib sheets through their leads, then aft to the jib winches. If the jib is no larger than 100 percent, the sheets may be run inside the shrouds. More likely the headsail will be a genoa with a relatively longer foot, which means that the sheet must be led outboard of the shrouds. Running genoa sheets inside the shrouds is among the most common errors by new sailors when rigging up the boat. But if you visualize the sail when it's up and drawing, you will recognize that the genoa, by definition, overlaps the mast, then you'll understand why its sheets must run outboard of the shrouds. Now with the jib ready to hoist, prepare the mainsail.

Some small-boat sailors leave the mainsail furled and covered on the boom. Others remove it after each sail and either roll or fold it to stow below. By causing creases, folding a sail (accordion-fashion is called flaking) tends to decrease its life span. Rolling, though something of a nuisance, is worth the effort with small (but still expensive) sails. If the main is furled and tied on the boom, remove the cover, but leave the sail ties on for now. Start the headboard up a foot or two in the luff groove on the back of the mast, and attach the halyard after making sure that it isn't wrapped around anything. Uncoil the mainsheet and pay it out on the cockpit sole such that it's free to run. Now both sails are ready to hoist.

Take a moment to walk around the deck inspecting the sheets and halyards. Will everything run clear when the sails are up and drawing? There is this immutable rule in sailing: If a line can hang up on something, it will. The best way to avoid screwups when rigging the boat for a sail is to establish a procedure, a mental or literal checklist, and stick to it until the process becomes second nature. Ask your crew to double-check everything.

Sit down at the helm, which will likely be a tiller, and take another minute to look around. Is your mainsheet really free to run? Though it's happened to us all at some point, it's no fun to sail away from a mooring, boats all around, only to discover that you can't ease the main because the sheet is knotted or wrapped around something. Have a look at the compass, and note the heading. Here at the mooring the compass and the bow will be pointing at the true wind, which we'll assume for now to be both steady and moderate, about 14 knots. All clear, you're ready to go sailing. Now you can decide whether to motor (assuming you have one) away from the mooring into open water—or to sail away. Let's sail away. (You can compromise by turning on the engine and leaving it in neutral, but ready to power you out of trouble should trouble arise.)

First (after removing the sail ties) hoist the main, but make sure before you do that there is no tension on the sheet; otherwise the boat might start sailing before you want it to. Just let the sail flap in the breeze. Be aware, though, that if the sail is flapping ("flogging" in more common usage), the boom will be bouncing around, and it can give you a sound crack on the head if you forget that fact. Then ask the bow person to stand ready to release the mooring line.

The mooring assembly, from the bottom up, consists typically of a mushroom-shaped anchor attached by chain to the mooring ball float. One end of the mooring line (called the pennant) is shackled to the top of the ball, and the other end is tied over or looped around a cleat on the foredeck. The boat end of the mooring line is rigged with a small float, like a lobster pot marker, and a tall fiberglass rod. Called a tall boy or a pickup, the float keeps the mooring line from sinking out of reach when not in use, and the rod offers a means of pulling the mooring line aboard the boat.

Okay, now you're ready to go. The main is up, the halyard cleated, but there is no tension on the sheet, which is clear to run. The bow person detaches the mooring pennant from the deck cleat and, pennant in hand, pulls the boat forward, thus placing the mooring ball on one side of the bow or the other. That done, he drops the pennant and the tall boy near the mooring ball. By that process you know where the gear is floating, lessening the chances of running over it, snagging your keel or rudder. The process will also tend to push the bow away from the gear, and that is the direction you want to head.

Harden up on the mainsheet, bringing the boom right up to the centerline. Turn the bow away from the mooring gear—and away from the wind. However, if you keep the main sheeted in tight as the bow bears away, the boat will not go forward; it will slide sideways. Ease away on the mainsheet to let the sail "breathe." It will soon begin to draw, and you'll feel the helm come alive in response to the boat's acceleration. Steer your way out of the mooring area into open water. Now you're ready to set the jib.

First poke the bow straight into the wind, ease well off on the sheet, and let the main flog over the centerline. Don't try to set the jib when sailing off the wind. There should be no trim on the jib as it's being set; both sheets should be loose. One of the crew steps to the mast and hauls hand-over-hand on the halyard. Don't trouble yourself about the degree of halyard tension at this point; just get the sail up. Now the jib, like the main, will be fluttering powerlessly along the centerline. This, for obvious reasons, is an undesirable state of sailing in which the boat is said to "in irons." To get out of irons, you essentially repeat the same tactic as when sailing away from the mooring. But it's even easier now with the headsail up. The jib trimmer, after taking a clockwise turn around the winch, hardens up on the sheet—the headsail, remember, wants to pull the bow away from the wind. If the headsail overlaps the mast, then harden up on the sheet on the overlapped side, and the sail will naturally pull the bow away from the wind. Meanwhile, the helmsman turns the bow in that same direction as the overlap.

BEAM REACHING

Steer the boat such that the apparent wind is blowing perpendicular to the centerline over the beam. Look up at the Windex. If the arrow is pointing toward the bow, then you need to come down. (If the wind is coming over the port side, for instance, then to come down, you turn right.) If the arrow is pointing toward the stern, then you need to steer up, toward the wind. Feel the breeze on the back of your neck, assuming that you're sitting up on the windward side, as you adjust the helm to bring the wind onto the beam. Ease the sheets on both sails until their luffs flutter, and then trim in just enough to stop the flutter. Now you have rough trim. Settle in and steer straight. Find a point on land and aim the bow at it. Is the wind still coming over the beam? If not, come up or down accordingly. Note the compass heading.

It's very tempting on a beam reach, perhaps more than on any other point of sail, to overtrim. Try to resist the temptation. If in doubt, as the saying goes, let it out. That applies to both sails. Experiment. Fiddle with the sails and with the helm. But, to repeat, make small adjustments, and only one at a time, noting its effect. If you have a speedometer, note the speed in tenths of a knot. But you don't need a speedo to know if you're accelerating or slowing. You can glean both from the feel of the apparent wind.

Now, what do you look at when sailing a straight line on a beam reach—or any other point of sail, for that matter? Don't look at any one thing exclusively, but get in the routine of letting your eyes rove around your various sources of information. Look at the Windex: Is it still pointing perpendicular to the centerline? Look at the telltales: Are they streaming? Look at your reference point on land. Look at the compass; it should be steady. Stay with it as long as you wish, until you get the feel.

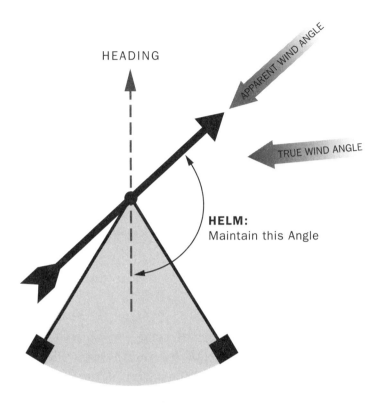

The Windex is a useful indicator because it always points toward the apparent wind.

What is the helm telling you? Many fin-keel boats in the 25-foot range (and most all dinghies) are steered by a tiller mounted directly on the transom-hung rudder. This, the simplest steering system, offers more palpable feedback than a wheel-steering system, which connects the wheel to the rudder by cables, but wheels are not inarticulate. You just have to "listen" more closely. The goal is to move the helm as little as possible. Rudders turn boats, but when you turn them off their fore-and-aft line, rudders also act as a brake. More important, though, a helm in need of constant adjustment to keep her going where you want indicates that the boat is out of balance and calling for trim adjustment. On a beam reach, chances are one sail or the other is overtrimmed. Try releasing the helm altogether. Does she maintain her heading? Does she want to come up? Fall down? The answer will tell you what sail to ease, what to tighten.

Remember that rough concept: The jib wants to pull the bow away from the wind, while the main wants to lever the bow to windward.

With this in mind, you can steer the boat with the sails alone, keeping the rudder amidships. If the bow tends to fall away from the wind, trim in the main slightly. If she tends to edge up toward the wind, trim in the jib. Experiment. Make small adjustments. (Reminder: While concentrating, on the visual and sensual information—while you have "your head in the boat," as they say—be sure to look outboard every now and then for traffic and obstructions.)

TAKING THE HELM

We've seen it numerous times when the new sailor is invited to steer, or "drive," in the slang. She clutches the helm as if it were a wild thing about to leap out of control causing something inscrutable but dreadful to happen, and, frozen, she peers straight ahead at nothing in particular. "Pick a point on land," suggests an experienced sailor, "and aim at it." So the new sailor pins her gaze on some point and refreezes, hoping that nothing changes. No, relax, nothing bad can happen in our 14-knot breeze. Steering a sailboat isn't all that difficult, but the best way to learn nothing is just to pick a point and steer for it. Instead, ask yourself the old question: Where is the wind?

Look at the Windex. It is indicating the sailing angle. Essentially, the helmsman's job is to maintain that angle. Sure, pick a point on land toward which the bow is pointing, but once you've done so, relinquish it, and feel the wind on your windward cheek and arm. If you feel the wind move from your windward cheek to the bridge of your nose, then you've gone off course. Look at the Windex—its angle will have changed. Look back at your land reference. Hold the tiller or wheel lightly, better to glean the signals offered by the helm. But perhaps the most useful suggestion for the new helmsman is to relax, try to dispense with performance anxiety, and experiment. Nothing bad can happen.

CLOSE REACHING

After you have the feel of the boat on the beam reach, try steering incrementally upwind to an apparent wind angle, as indicated by the Windex, of about 45 degrees; that's somewhere between a beam reach and a beat—a close reach. But go up slowly; try making the turn in concert with the jib trimmer, leaving him time to trim in as you turn. The same applies to the main. On small boats, the helmsman is also the main trimmer, because the mainsheet will be positioned near the helm. But you don't have to do this. Someone else can sit beside the helm and trim the main while you concentrate on steering. Strive to trim—hardening up on the sheets in this case— so that you keep the tales streaming as you turn toward the wind. Smooth, slow, and easy—you don't need to rush yourself.

Once you're up at 45 degrees apparent, settle back in and absorb the new feel. The apparent wind, you notice, has increased. Do you feel windward pressure on the helm? It's that weather helm we discussed earlier, a sort of imbalance in the interaction of forces among sails, hull, and keel. This is not necessarily undesirable in that it lends the helm some feel, which in turn helps the helmsman keep a steady course. Some boats carry neutral helms (no feel; you have to consciously steer them all the time). In that case, precise steering requires a bit more concentration. But if your arm is getting tired fighting the weather helm, then there is too much, and you'll want to "soften" the helm. Try easing the traveler down slightly below centerline. Lowering the traveler, remember, spills wind from the mainsail. You could also induce twist (cause the upper part of the leech to fall away from, and therefore, spill wind.

When a boat heels excessively, as in a gust, she tends to "round up" toward the wind—in other words, heeling causes weather helm. To explain why would require a digression into hydrodynamic theory, an interesting subject, but not one absolutely necessary to learning to sail. Suffice it to say that when the boat heels, the round, wide bilge enters the water, detrimentally altering the shape of the object trying to pass through the water. The new shape presented to the water and the altered forces of wind in the sail plan cause the bow to pivot up into the wind—and recognizing this fact, that excessive heeling causes the boat to round up, is necessary to learning to sail. As a novice helmsperson, you can use that tendency to your advantage. You don't need to fight the helm to keep her down in the gusts. Just let the boat go where she is trying to head. The weather helm caused by the heeling will, by rounding the boat into the wind, spill wind force from the sails.

Lee helm—the tendency to turn away from the wind—is less common than weather helm and less desirable. If a weather-helmed boat is left to her own devices, the worst that can happen is that she slips into irons. A lee-helmed boat, sliding away from the wind, will eventually find the wind pushing at 90 degrees against the sails (trimmed in tight for a beat), and all the wind's force will be directed to pushing her over.

New sailors tend to be nervous about changing things. Don't worry; go right ahead and fiddle with the sheets. But be sure to watch the sails as you ease or tighten their sheets. Look up. Look outside the boat to make sure you're not about to hit anything, then look back up. You'll learn to sail by looking up. Try turning the helm a few degrees one way or the other without changing trim, and watch what happens in the sails. Note the jib telltales— one or the other will droop, depending on which way you turn in relation to the wind. The tales in the main leech will flop to one side of the sail or the other. You're now out of trim because you changed the sailing angle without making commensurate changes in the angle of the sails. Steer back to the original heading until the tales stream again. The point of the little exercise is to demonstrate an unwavering principle of sailing. If the wind angle changes, either because you turn the boat or because the wind shifts, then the sails will need to be tightened or eased accordingly.

Sailing a straight line, get in the habit of looking astern at your wake. Is it straight? If not, concentrate on your helming until you leave a straight wake. Add looking astern to the visual checklist that includes telltales, Windex, compass, and land reference. Also, teach yourself to notice waves. Even when they're small, waves will affect your track through the water. And you can use the waves to indicate the true wind direction, since it will almost always be perpendicular to the wave face. Compare that direction with the apparent wind direction indicated by the Windex.

AN ASIDE: LEE HELM

There are more J/24s in the world than any other small keelboats. If you can win national-level races in J/24s, then you have a future as a professional sailor. The boat is nimble and quick, a little sports car, but the design, the first in the incredibly successful J/Boat line, is not perfect. She carries a degree of lee helm; the bow naturally wants to fall away from the wind. You can compensate for this with the helm, but that requires turning the rudder off the centerline, which slows the boat. No, you have to compensate for the lee helm with the sails, not the rudder. You do that by easing way off on the luff tension with the halyards. You want to see wrinkles in the luffs of the genoa and main. You have to make the sails look ugly. A "soft" luff in the main, remember, moves the draft position aft. In other words, much of the wind's force is directed toward the back of the main. This in turn pushes the back of the boat away from the wind, turning the bow toward the wind, thus obviating the lee helm. You've compensated for a design imbalance by reshaping the sail to attain renewed balance. A little lee helm doesn't make a particle of difference when you're out for leisurely daysail, only when racing. However, for educational purposes, note the concept—that you can balance, even steer the boat by adjusting both the shape of the sails and their angles to the apparent wind direction. When the sails are balanced, the helm becomes a means of gentle correction, not coercion.

BEATING

There are only a few degrees' difference between a close reach and a full-on beat. Turn up slowly, trimming in on the main and jib simultaneously. The apparent wind will increase markedly. Sit up on the windward side and look at your sails. They're hauled in tight, the telltales streaming on jib and main. Now fiddle. Ease one sail, say the jib, until the luff begins to flutter slightly and the inside telltale droops. Take it back in until the flutter stops and the tales stream. Keep the helm steady while doing so.

Now pull hard on the mainsheet until the leech begins to curl ("hook") to windward, and the leech telltales point to windward. That's too tight. Ease slightly on the sheet until the leech straightens and the tales stream aft. Now crouch down beneath the boom and sight up to the top batten in the main. In ideal wind/trim conditions, the top batten and the boom should be parallel. If not—if, say, the outboard end of the batten angles to leeward relative to the boom—then you probably need a little more leech tension. Keep in mind that, when sailing on the wind, the mainsheet is pulling nearly straight down on the leech, and that makes it a "leech control." Tightening it "closes"

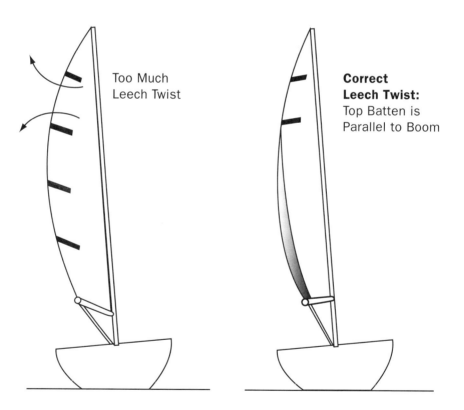

Too Much
Leech Twist

**Correct
Leech Twist:**
Top Batten is
Parallel to Boom

Sometimes leech twist is desirable—but not when sailing to windward in light air. In that case, tighten the sheet until the top batten is parallel to the boom.

the leech, while easing it "opens" the leech. The leech of the main on this point of sail is acting as a rudder. When you tighten the leech, the boat will tend to ease into the wind.

Notice your degree of heel when sailing to windward by gauging the angle of the headstay in relation to the land or the horizon. Try to keep that angle constant when sailing in a straight line.

Notice, too, the relationship between the vertical curve in the leech of the jib and the vertical curve of the main at the point where the jib overlaps it. The curves should be parallel. A 100 percent jib does not overlap the main, but the jib leech will still be curved. See that it conforms to the curve in the mainsail leech. Remember, the two sails, while doing separate work, are acting in concert. The collaboration is particularly active and efficacious at that point where the headsail and main overlap as with genoas, called the slot. If you "close" the slot too much by overtrimming the genoa, then the wind will be directed by the leech of the jib into the back of the main. This will cause a noticeable bulge on the windward side of the main. We don't want that. We want to let the wind to benefit us as it passes through the slot. Likewise, if you undertrim the genoa and the leech separates from the main, then the airflow falls away to leeward instead of flowing smoothly off the genoa leech onto the back of the main. Stick with the telltales—if everything is streaming, then chances are the slot will be working efficiently.

What essentially you're doing fiddling with the sails and helm is searching for the groove, the optimum balance of forces—wind around the sails, water around the keel, when sailing to windward. When you have her in the groove, the boat will tell you. You'll feel a little surge of joy when you first find that groove and the boat suddenly expresses her pleasure. You'll recognize that your original impulse to take up sailing because it might be fun was entirely justified. And from then on you'll know without doubt whether and when you're in the groove.

For now, the objective is to stay in the groove. Conditions change constantly. The wind gusts and lulls and shifts its direction. Still, if you follow your telltales, you'll likely remain in the groove. Stay with it for a while, sailing a straight line and focusing on nothing but the telltales on the jib

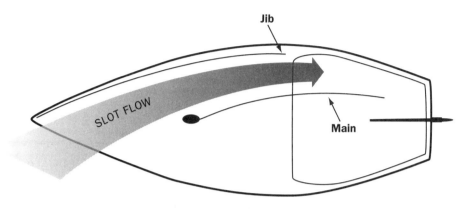

Think of the main and jib as a single wing unified by the cooperation that occurs between the windward side of the jib and the leeward side of the main—the slot. The curves in both sails must be parallel.

luff. Keep the tales on the windward and leeward side of the sail streaming in unison. If the inside tale droops, then bear away ever so slightly until it streams again. If the outside tale droops, then you're sailing too low. You might find it useful on a tiller-steered boat to address the too-high-too-low question in these terms: Move the tiller toward the telltale that is luffing. If the "far" one is luffing, assuming you're sitting to windward, push the tiller away from you, to leeward, to bring the bow closer to the wind. If you're pinching (windward tale luffing), pull the tiller toward you, toward the windward side of the boat. With practice, these movements will soon become second nature. To a significant extent, the sails are steering the boat when sailing to windward. And with both sails properly trimmed, the boat will likely hold a straight course if you release the helm.

If you didn't need three people on the windward rail to keep her flat on a close reach, you might need their weight when close-hauled, depending of course on the apparent wind velocity. Position the traveler such that the boom is on the centerline. But if this move significantly increases heel, then lower the boom back below centerline. Check the telltales on the mainsail leech. They should be streaming aft. On some mainsails, when optimally trimmed, the upper telltale will flutter about 50 percent of the time.

If your headsail is bigger than 100 percent and its foot "sweeps" along the deck, you won't be able to see what's going on to leeward. If you're sailing on port tack, you have no rights, so somebody had better go periodically to the low side and look "below" you for traffic. You have right-of-way on starboard tack, but don't take it for granted. You still need to look outside the boat. Don't forget as you concentrate on steering and trimming, enjoying the groove, that you're moving. Nothing ruins a fine sailing day more thoroughly than a collision or grounding.

Note the compass heading. Find a new land reference whenever you put in a helm adjustment. Check the new Windex angle. It will be pointing toward the bow at a sharp angle, but remember that you're steering to the apparent wind, which is at its strongest on a beat. And the true wind is well aft of the Windex angle in relation to centerline. Waves, which indicate the true wind, will also tend to knock your bow around. If there is a tidal current setting against the wind, then the waves will tend to be steeper and "shorter" (the distance between crests) than if wind and current were both heading in the same direction, even in 14 to 15 knots of true wind. Steady breeze and flat seas—these are ideal conditions for small-boat sailing in general and, specifically, for learning to feel the boat and the wind. But since water is sailing's medium, waves will be a fact of life. Here's the rule of thumb when beating into the waves: Steer up on the face of the wave and down the back of the wave. This is easy to say, but it takes practice to accomplish. However, still again, you can learn a lot by simply observing the waves. Chances are, they'll be pretty consistent, and by observing them you'll be able to anticipate their impact on your bow.

When sailing to windward, you'll experience some degree of leeway. All sailboats slide sideways as they go to windward, some more than others depending on design factors and wind velocity. Leeway is negligible on a beam reach, nonexistent on a run, and at its most powerful on a beat. You can't really feel it happening, but you can see it happening when you know what to look for. We're talking here about the difference between the direction the boat is moving through the water and its direction over the bottom. In other words, your bow will be pointing in one direction, but you won't actually be going in that direction. You're going, instead, at an angle downwind of that direction: leeway. Check your wake. If you're making a lot of leeway, your wake will angle away to windward.

Current is the other, greater force affecting your course over the ground. In inshore waters, current is usually caused by tides. See chapter 8 for more about tides and current sailing, wherein we'll discuss how to gauge visually the relationship between your apparent course and your course actually "made good" over the bottom. But for now, remember to seek out indicators of current while you're sailing. Current will form a wake around any object fixed to the bottom—lobster pots, mooring balls, navigation buoys, etc. The extent of the wake will signal the velocity of the tidal current, and its orientation will tell you the direction of the flow. This, too, is part of learning to observe the environment through a sailor's eyes.

Okay, let's look back at the sails. Beating, they're sheeted in as close to the centerline as possible. The boom is centered by means of the traveler. The main leech is tight, but not hooked to windward, and the telltales on the leech are streaming. So are the telltales near the luff of the jib. Notice, when you're in the groove, the spatial relationship between the jib leech and the tip of the leeward spreader. The leech will be about 4 inches off the spreader, depending on the boat and the sail. Generally, though, this distance will serve as another good indicator of optimum windward trim. Now sail the boat in a straight line, circle the rig with your eyes, feel the wind on your cheek. Absorb sensation. Sailboats are particularly communicative when close-hauled.

WINDWARD SAILING

When they first feel a boat on a beat as the apparent wind surges, the deck turns into a steep hillside, and the sheets load up, some new sailors blanch. Some people simply cannot put their faith in the fact that the designer has built stability into the boat; they're unable to feel the boat's form stability kick in as she heels. And chances are, if you're at the helm, the first time the boat heels hard you won't be focusing coolly on leech tension and traveler position. Telltales? What telltales? Don't pressure yourself. If you feel anxious, give the helm if possible to a more experienced sailor. Sit back, relax, and observe. However, recognize this for now: Despite the increased apparent, the feel of high speed, you are not at risk of losing control of the boat when sailing on the wind. All you need to do is throw off the sheets. The sails will flog and the boat will slow. Or just turn up into the eye of the wind, and the same thing will happen.

If you are out for a daysail or a weekend cruise, you probably will not apply such close attention to sail trim as we're discussing in this chapter. And as you gain experience, you'll be able to find the windward groove, for instance, without devoting race-boat attention to trim and weight placement. However, at this early stage in the learning process, seize every opportunity to sail "seriously," which is to say concentrate on nothing but the sail trim, the helm, and the feel of the boat and the wind on your face. Do so for short periods, then relax and sail more casually. You might take the jib down and tool around under main alone for a while. Any time spent in the boat will be useful. Take it easy, talk things through with your mates, but then, when you feel like it, regain your concentration and sail "seriously," concentrating on your telltales and the other indicators. But by all means at this early stage don't pressure yourself. Just by being aboard you'll gain valuable experience (no matter the point of sail) that you might not recognize as such at the time. But it's still money in the bank of experience.

BROAD REACHING

You've been sailing close-hauled on port tack (the wind has been blowing over the port bow; the jib is sheeted on the starboard side). Now let's bear off—in other words, turn the boat away from the wind. Here is a chance to perform a revealing experiment. Leave the sails strapped in for a beat and try to turn away from the wind. She won't go down; she'll fight to stay up. This is because of the fundamental dynamic in a sloop between headsail and mainsail. The main wants to lever the boat up to windward—that in a real sense is its job.

To release the pressure, ease away on the mainsheet. Then turn the boat to the right to bear away from a port tack. (If you turn the other way from a port tack, you would cross the eye of the wind; you would tack, and for now we're not going to do that.) If you leave the jib trimmed in for the beat as you turn the boat, the wind will help you turn by pushing against the sail. You'll go down quite quickly. Then ease away on the jib. (Don't forget to look for traffic before you make the turn. And don't change your point of sail until you're ready and all aboard know what you're planning to do.) Our objective is to turn such that the apparent wind blows over the port quarter, that is, at an angle to the centerline of about 150 degrees. But let's not do it all at once.

Straighten the boat when you arrive back at a beam reach. Watch your Windex. It is the most useful indicator as you're turning. Settle in again, steer straight, trim your sails according to the telltales, and don't give in to that temptation to overtrim. Feel the boat accelerate. (Lacking momentum, small boats slow down much more quickly than big boats, but they also accelerate more quickly.) Keeping the rudder amidships, see if you can make her go faster by fiddling, one adjustment at a time, with the sail trim. Notice the apparent wind, not only its visual angle reflected by the Windex, but the feel of it as well on your face or exposed arm. Your apparent wind is about to drop precipitously.

Turn slowly away from the wind, watching your Windex as you do so. Ease away on the main and jib sheets. It will be very easy to turn past a broad reach onto a run. If you're sitting on the windward side facing inboard, the apparent will move onto the back of your neck. Straighten her out at any point along the way as you edge the apparent wind over the port quarter. Everything will feel different now compared with the beat. The boat seems to sag down in the water. She won't respond as nimbly to the helm. Maybe you felt a little chilly when you were beating to windward. If you put on a windbreaker, you'll probably want to take it off now that you're on a broad reach. And this brings us back to that fundamental principle of sailing:

When the apparent is forward of the beam, the wind circulates on both sides of the sails. They are behaving like that airplane wing, generating lift as a result of differences in air pressure on the windward and leeward sides. At this stage in your learning process, we might simplify the concept by saying that, when the wind is forward of the beam, the sails are pulling the boat along. But as you turn downwind and ease the sails out, the wind cannot effectively reach the leeward side of the sails. Therefore, the wind is pushing the boat. Lift is being generated on a beam reach, but lift diminishes as you turn farther downwind. So when the apparent goes well aft of the beam to a broad reach, there are two factors militating against fast, fun sailing. One is the decreased apparent wind; the other is decreased efficiency of the sails. Look at your jib. It's suffocating in the lee of the main, hanging limp, quite nearly useless. This is not merely decreased efficiency; this is no efficiency.

To examine the concept in other terms, consider broad reaching in good stiff true wind of 20 knots. That's quite sufficient to push a light keelboat at a good speed, say, 6 knots, maybe more. If we were sailing upwind in that breeze, our small keelboat, her sails, and her crew would be experiencing something around 24 knots. That's a lot. Overpowered, we'd need to shorten sail or take other measures to spill some of that wind force from the sails. However, in our 14 knots of true wind, downwind sailing is pretty sluggish. The main telltales won't stream. The helm doesn't feel like it has the same firm bite on the water as when we were sailing on the wind, because it doesn't. A rudder works only when water is streaming over its surfaces, and it works best when water is streaming quickly. Now the helm probably feels unresponsive, sort of slushy.

Let the main out as far as it can go. Notice whether the center of the sail is chafing against the leeward shroud and spreader tip. If so, you might as well pull it in enough to prevent that. You might be slightly overtrimmed after doing so—the wind should meet the sail at a 90-degree angle—but this point of sail is far less trim-sensitive than upwind sailing, because the wind is meeting only one side of the sail. We lack lift. Just to exercise the principle, let's ask: How do I reestablish lift? You have to turn back up at least far enough up to initiate flow over the jib. But if your "destination" lay downwind, then you'll no longer be pointing at it. There's the problem. If you stay down at a broad reach, the boat will be slow; if you come up far enough to establish flow over both sides of the sails, then you will be sailing away from your destination.

RUNNING

This is the next and final increment down from a broad reach. You are said to be running when the wind is blowing over the transom along the centerline. In other words, the wind is dead aft. If you allow the wind to move past the centerline onto the same side of the boat as the mainsail, you are said to be sailing by the lee.

If you continue in that direction, the wind will eventually find the leeward side of the main, and it will jibe. We'll talk about jibing in the next chapter, but jibes must be controlled. And the best way to avoid an accidental jibe is to avoid sailing by the lee (or, some people would suggest, avoid running dead downwind). When sailing with the apparent wind angle dead

Sailing by the Lee

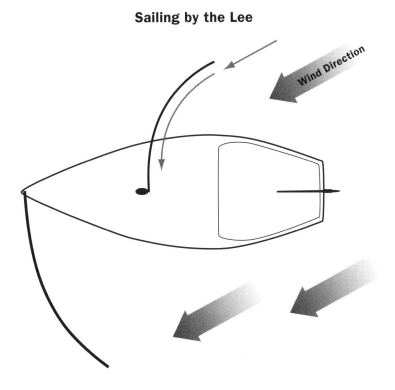

Sailing downwind, if the wind blows over the same side of the boat as the mainsail, then you're sailing "by the lee."

from behind and with the mainsail far out on one side or the other, pause to think about which way you need to turn to avoid the jibe. You'll need to turn toward the wind, to come up. If the wind is blowing over the transom, however, you might get confused about which way is windward. On a tiller-steered boat, if you put the tiller toward the mainsail, you will come up no matter the point of sail you start from. If you put the tiller away from the main, you will go down. Another mechanistic way to think about it is that if you find yourself sailing by the lee, turning the boat a few degrees away from the mainsail will bring you up. With practice, find that you no longer need to think in mechanistic terms as the moves become second nature. It often happens all of a sudden. "Hey," you realize on day, "I did the right thing without having to cogitate.

Their broad efficiency notwithstanding, sloops suffer downwind, because the jib smothers in the lee of the mainsail. Sure, you can pull the jib out on the side opposite the boom—"wing-and-wing"—and it's good practice to do so, since it requires attentive steering to keep both sails drawing. For that same reason, sailing wing-and-wing is not a practical, sustained solution to the downwind problem. And it's especially difficult to keep a big genoa flying wing-and-wing, since there is nothing to support its clew except the diminished apparent wind. (When sailing long distances downwind, some sailors use a pole, the inboard end fixed to the mast, to hold the jib clew out to weather.) Just when you need greater sail area to compensate for the deeply decreased apparent wind, you essentially lose your headsail.

On a dead run, the boom will be eased outboard as far as the shrouds allow. (And of course if you choose to wing the jib, it will be flying on the opposite side.) That means that the mainsheet is lying almost horizontally between the boat and the boom, in which case the sheet is unable to exert any downward pull on the boom. This allows the aft end of the boom to ride up as the wind pushes on the middle of the main. Another way to say it is that the mainsheet has ceased to be a leech control, so the leech is now free to fall off to leeward, rendering the main even less efficient. Haul on the boom vang to bring the boom parallel to the water surface. This will tighten the leech, thus retaining rather than spilling wind from the mainsail, and tightening the vang will prevent the aft end of the boom from bouncing around.

SPINNAKERS

I contend that the new sailor has enough that is esoteric and unfamiliar to grasp and to practice and that, therefore, spinnakers and their handling are best left to a later stage in the learning process. However, since we're talking about downwind sailing, we can't ignore the sail that exists solely to address the inherent problem in downwind sailing—that lack of sail area to compensate for the decrease in apparent wind.

There are two versions—the symmetrical spinnaker and the simpler asymmetrical spinnaker. The latter (usually shortened to asym) is really a great billowing genoa. Though the luff flies free of the headstay, an asym has a tack, clew, and head just like a genoa. However, because it's tacked to the bow, the asym cannot work well when the wind is much aft of the beam for the same reason a genoa doesn't work on deep points of sail—the main blankets it. The asymmetrical spinnaker really comes into its own when beam reaching or nearly broad reaching. When the wind is on the quarter, at about a 150-degree angle to the centerline, the asym begins to sag in the lee of the main.

The symmetrical spinnaker (you'll hear it called the 'chute or kite) solves that problem. It does so by presenting sail area out on the opposite side of the boat from the main. Spinnakers have no tack, only a head and two symmetrical clews. The windward clew of the spinnaker is connected to a dedicated pole fixed perpendicular to the mast. This pole, by supporting the corner of the sail, allows you to project a lot of sail area out on the windward side of the boat. You can, therefore, sail "deeper" angles and go faster downwind. You pay a price, however.

As the illustration shows, you need additional running rigging (a downhaul and a topping lift) to control the pole, plus a fitting on the mast to accommodate the inboard end of the pole. Because they are both large and complicated, spinnakers tend to fly out of control unless carefully tended to. Spinnakers can make good crews look like a ship of fools. Plus, you need additional, experienced crew to hoist

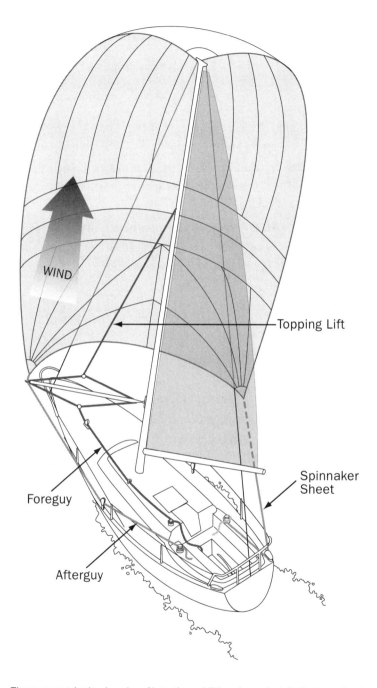

The symmetrical spinnaker. Note the additional running rigging required.

the spinnaker and another to tend the clew control lines (one running through the end of the pole, the other flying free) to keep the 'chute flying. To take down, or "douse" the spinnaker, requires someone to ease the halyard in concert with another crew hauling all that nylon back aboard, plus the helmsman. Even experienced crew can screw up the douse, in which case the expensive sail becomes a great sea anchor—just before it shreds. It's happened to us all at some point, and it's quite the show when spinnakers whip out of control, but one best watched from another boat.

I should add, however, since we've been dwelling on their complexity and demands on the crew, that nothing in sailing is more fun than blasting along in an adrenaline rush with a stiff breeze filling a big spinnaker. But try to have the experience first as a passenger on a well-crewed boat.

On a dead run pay close attention to your Windex, which should be pointing aft right down the centerline. Even experienced sailors find it challenging to steer dead down without using the Windex as a visual reference, because in the diminished apparent it is difficult to feel the wind. If the Windex points off the centerline, steer the boat away from the arrowhead to correct your heading. Or if you prefer, steer the boat back under the arrow. On this point of sail, it's especially important to make small helm changes and wait for them to take effect. You don't want to jibe until you mean to. If the Windex points toward the mainsail, then you are sailing by the lee, and you want to steer the boat away from the boom/mainsail. Steering away from the boom will always bring you up closer to the wind, thus away from the jibe. Whenever you steer down anywhere near the jibe, remind all those aboard to watch their heads.

Remember also that waves can cause an accidental jibe by kicking the stern under the mainsail. The boat behaves differently in waves when sailing to windward than when running. On a beat, the boat is driving through the

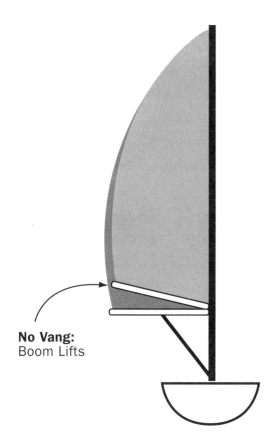

Sailing downwind, the boom vang acts as a leech control, preventing the mainsail leech from falling away to leeward and spilling air.

No Vang:
Boom Lifts

waves. On a run, she is riding atop the waves, then sagging into their troughs, a less stable condition. The boat might pivot on the crests, thus changing the apparent wind angle. You need to help the boat keep her bow pointing where you want more actively on a dead run than on a beat. But to practice this you don't have to sail dead down so close to an accidental jibe. Turn up a few degrees to put the wind over the windward stern quarter to give yourself a little more room for error. Again, your Windex is the best indicator of apparent wind angle, but don't pin your eyes exclusively on the arrow. That will likely lead to confusion. When running, unlike when beating, your boat is not making leeway. And in the absence of current, your boat is heading exactly where the bow is pointing. Find a prominent land reference and shift your eyes from that point up to the Windex, and around again.

WEIGHT IN THE REAL WORLD

Light boats are more fun to sail than heavy boats. And because they're quicker, nimbler, and more responsive to the helm and changes in sail trim, lighter boats are better to learn on.

I've heard people sailing heavy, undercanvased clunkers claim that they'd rather give up a few knots of boatspeed in exchange for their family's safety in a heavy boat when a storm blows in. This argument doesn't hold up in the real world. Unless you sail in San Francisco Bay, Key West in winter, or the English Channel, the sailing problem will be lack of wind, not too much of it. Further, heavy weather doesn't blow inexplicably. It's associated with large-scale frontal movement, which is widely predicted in newspapers, on TV, and on the Web. National Oceanographic and Atmospheric Administration (NOAA, "Noah") weather forecasts are available twenty-four hours a day on channels one and two on your VHF radio, and you're required by the Coast Guard to carry a VHF. In other words, there is no reason to be caught out in a "storm." The best way to protect your family from heavy weather is to stay home when it's due. By the way, most of those clunker sailors wind up trading the boat for a light, slippery boat with a healthy sail area. Or, growing bored with dull performance and limited range, they quit sailing altogether.

6

THE MANEUVERS

ET'S DEFINE MANEUVERS AS TURNS REQUIRING EITHER the bow or the stern to pass through the eye of the wind. There are two versions: the jibe and the tack. In a jibe the stern crosses the eye of the wind. In a tack, the bow crosses the wind's eye. Thus, jibing is associated with downwind sailing, tacking with upwind sailing. Let's look at both maneuvers separately in their contexts of upwind and downwind sailing.

UPWIND: THE TACK

Stick the bow directly into the wind. The sails flap like flags; the boat slows and stops. This is what we mean by the "eye of the wind." You go from one tack to the other by passing, without stopping, through the wind's eye. Let's describe the tack itself, and then talk about when to tack and about some of subtleties of windward sailing.

Put the boat starboard tack. Remember, a boat is said to be on starboard tack (or abbreviated to "on starboard") when the apparent wind blows over the starboard bow. That means, of course, that the jib is drawing on the port side, the leeward side. Sheet in the main and jib. Make the telltales fly. Then settle in, feel the boat, and notice the angle of the apparent wind as indicated by the Windex. The objective of the tack is to transfer—by turning the boat—that same apparent wind angle to the opposite bow. If you're fortunate enough to have a dinghy to practice on, you can execute the tack yourself. But let's stick with our small keelboat in the following discussion, and assume the presence of a helmsman—you—and at least one crew, a jib trimmer. In that case, the dialogue will go something like this:

"Ready about?" you ask.

"Ready," replies the jib trimmer. Ready means that the trimmer has made certain that the tail of the active sheet is free to run, and he has the lazy sheet positioned with one turn around the winch ready to be hauled in on the new windward side.

"Hard alee," you say as you turn bow into the wind. (You don't have to say "hard alee" or "helm's alee." You can say whatever you wish, but say it consistently to alert the crew, after asking if they are ready, that you're initiating the tack.)

When the jib begins to luff in the eye of the wind, the trimmer throws the active sheet off the winch or detaches it from the cleat, and lets it run.

Meanwhile, the driver steers the boat—in a single motion—through the eye of the wind until it blows over the port bow. It's best to center the traveler before the tack, but you need not adjust the main trim. The main will tack itself. Once you've crossed the eye of the wind, the jib trimmer sheets in the sail on the starboard side.

You've tacked. It is not a complicated maneuver, and it is a lot safer, as you'll see, than a jibe. But you can't learn to tack or jibe a sailboat from a book. Only practice will solidify the actual technique, but it can be usefully described along with some of the issues involved. If you're steering with a wheel, the technique is simple—just turn the wheel to windward. If the boat is tiller-steered, you'll have to work out how to move around the tiller and the traveler. Ideally, you'll do so while continuing to face forward watching the jib transition from side to side and the bow as you turn. This involves lifting the tiller to pass it behind your back, and, while the move isn't particularly difficult, the only way to learn to do it is to tack and tack and tack again. That's the basic maneuver. Now let's go back and look more closely at the tacking procedure.

BEFORE YOU TACK

Look around for traffic to windward. If you have any doubt about what the boats nearby are doing or going to do, just hold your course (starboard beat, in this case) until you're sure you'll be clear after the tack. Then pick some point of land lying away at about a 90-degree angle to your centerline. That's roughly where your bow will be pointing when you complete the tack. The aft face of your cabin trunk, which "crosses" the centerline of the boat at 90 degrees, is a useful sightline to estimate where you'll be heading after the tack. Take a moment to visualize the maneuver, bearing in mind that if you don't steer fully through the eye of the wind, the boat will stop ("in irons") with the sails fluttering uselessly. Now you're ready to go. Inform the crew of that fact: "Ready about?" "Ready to tack?" Center your traveler. Then turn the boat.

HOW FAST SHOULD YOU TURN?

That will depend on the size of the boat and the size of the headsail. Because they carry more momentum, larger keelboats can be eased through the tack, while on small centerboard boats, you might need to shove the helm over assertively. If you're carrying a 135 percent genoa with a small crew, then the driver shouldn't turn the boat faster than the trimmer can haul the sail around the mast. If the driver out-turns the trimmer, then, when the tack is complete, the headsail will be out beyond the lifelines way undertrimmed, and she'll have to grind it in against the force of the wind. The trimmer should try to keep the foot of the headsail inside the lifelines during the tack, and the driver should time the speed of the tack accordingly. This is of course not an issue with a 100 percent jib.

HOW DO YOU KNOW WHEN TO STOP TURNING THE BOAT?

Wind awareness. Where is the wind? When the tack is complete, you should be sailing the same apparent wind angle as you were before the tack, only on the opposite side of the boat. Yes, that's the objective, but you don't want to stop the turn when you reach that same wind angle. You want to steer a few degrees below that wind angle before you stop the turn. Here's why:

Because they are trying to move against the wind (and waves), boats slow down considerably through the tacks. If you stop your turn when you arrive at the wind angle at which the boat was sailing up to speed on the old tack, the sails will stall, the boat will sag and slow. Instead, bear away toward a close reach as you come out of the tack. The same principle applies to the jib trimmer. Instead of immediately trimming the sail as tightly on the new tack as when in the groove on the old tack, he should leave it somewhat undertrimmed. That distance between the luff of the jib and the spreader tip is a useful indicator. Perhaps leave the sail out twice the distance as when the boat was sailing on the old tack to let the sail breathe. Wait to feel the boat accelerate. If you have a speedometer, watch the numbers climb, but don't pin your eyes on the speedo. Then simultaneously trim in the jib as you turn the boat back up to a beat and feel for the groove. It's one smooth motion, a carved turn through the wind and out the other side low of a full beat, then gradually back up to a beat.

IN THE REAL WORLD

There is risk here of making the tack too complicated. Turn the boat through the wind's eye, pull the jib across, straighten out the boat—you've tacked. That's how most people out for a daysail or a weekend cruise tack their boats. Most don't studiously bear away when coming out of the tack, sails eased, then carve the turn back up to a beat as they trim main and jib in unison. Nothing wrong with that. Once you learn to perform the maneuvers, you can decide for yourself how finely you want to execute them.

However, for the sake for the principle, it might be worth mentioning that racers, when coming out of a light-air tack, regain speed lost in the turn by "shifting gears." In low gear, when acceleration is the objective, the helmsman bears away, the trimmers ease the sheets. As the boat accelerates, they shift incrementally into a higher gear by trimming in and pointing up until they arrive back at the same speed, trim, and sailing angle as when on the old tack. In heavier air, it's not necessary to bear away as far or wait as long changing gears as the boat re-accelerates. You probably won't be able to pull this off in your early practice sessions. (Not all race crews manage to accelerate consistently out of the tack by shifting gears.) Don't worry about it. Practice turning the boat through the eye of the wind and pulling the jib through the fore triangle. Just get the physical moves down. Yet at the same time, keep the principle in the back of your mind: In slow conditions, bear away from the wind, ease the sheets, and let the sails breathe. Then as you feel the speed build, trim in and edge the boat back up to a beat.

In the real world, you might find yourself disoriented as the bow swings through the wind. Most new sailors steer the boat way too far downwind after completing the tack, and suddenly they realize they're sailing on a beam reach when they meant to come out of the tack on a close reach. If that happens to you, worry not. No harm done. Collect yourself, check your Windex, and then at your leisure turn her back up toward the wind, trimming for the beat.

One reason sailors get confused as they tack the boat through the eye of the wind is that the turn seems so damn big. It is big, usually about 90 degrees. The source of confusion is that trick played by the apparent wind. When beating, the apparent wind angle looks very tight. The Windex is pointing almost at the bow; it looks like you're sailing at about a 20-degree angle to the wind. And if the objective of the tack is to shift that same angle from, say, the starboard bow to the port bow, well, then that looks to require only a small turn. And that's the trick—it's the apparent wind angle you're observing, not the true angle. The true angle is well aft of that indicated by the Windex. (Check the waves for a reminder of the true wind angle.) And you are not actually sailing anywhere near that close to the true wind. So to the new sailor it seems to take forever to get the bow through the wind. Something's wrong, but what? Confusion overcomes thinking, and the boat just keeps turning. Again, no harm done. Just recognize what's actually going on, and learn from the mistake. Steer her back up to windward.

A good way to avoid surprise at the size of the turn is, as mentioned before, to look to windward before you tack for a land feature, a target, away at about 90 degrees to your centerline. With practice, you'll be able to refine your choice of target and the steering required to hit it. Tack, tack, tack. Pause between tacks only to get the boat back up to the same speed and angle as on the old tack. Then go again. Switch places with the jib trimmer, and tack some more. When you get tired of working, take a break. If you find an experienced boat owner willing to let you practice like that on her boat—and help your correct errors—buy the good person dinner, express your appreciation, and ask when you can do it again.

TACKING TO GET SOMEWHERE

So far we've been talking about tacking for its own sake, as a mechanical maneuver. Once you acquire enough practice to execute the maneuver, start thinking about how to reach and round an upwind destination by tacking. For a "destination," pick an object anchored to the bottom about half a mile away to windward. A navigation buoy will serve—unless the buoy marks a rock ledge or other obstruction and unless it marks one side of a busy channel. A lobster pot buoy will do, or if the water isn't too deep, you could make your own mark with a weight, line, and float. Choose an uncrowded stretch of water, if possible, where there will be no crossing situations to deal with. Now put the boat on a beat. Let's start, arbitrarily, on starboard tack. And let's decide, equally arbitrarily, that you want round the upwind mark "to port." In other words, as you sail around the mark, it will lie on the port side of the boat.

Again, go through all the routines for straight-line sailing. Remember your visual aids—the Windex, the telltales, the distance between the leech of the jib and the spreader tip, and a land reference—as you trim it up. Keep going until you find the groove, then settle in. Now notice the angular relationship between the boat's heading and your upwind mark. You're gaining on it, but not of course heading toward it. Note the compass heading. The compass will be useful in this your first windward leg and the many others to follow. Get used to reading and making sense of the compass as soon as possible. You don't want to pin your eyes on it, a temptation as you're getting to know the compass, but include it in your "roving eye" glimpse at all the visual aids.

"Ready about?"

"Ready here."

"Helm's alee."

You've tacked onto port. Once you get her trimmed up and sailing close-hauled, look again at your mark. Does port tack bring you closer to the mark than starboard? If so, that will be the "favored tack," and you'll spend more time on that "board" than on the other. If you're not sure, put in two more tacks, and look again. If the mark you've chosen lies dead upwind, then there will be no favored tack, but keep looking at the relation between your sailing angle and the mark. Soon you will begin to understand the geometry of upwind sailing. You are of course zigzagging toward your mark. If your target mark lies directly upwind and if the wind direction does not shift, you'll spend an equal time on port and starboard tacks to reach your mark. However, the windward angle you gain on each tack will depend on several factors.

HOW HIGH CAN YOU POINT?

Windward capability varies widely from boat to boat. Obviously, a race boat with new sails and a crack crew will point higher than a mom-and-pop cruising boat with five seasons on her sails. (Sails stretch over time depending on the material used in their construction, their "mileage," and their owner's care and maintenance.) In any case, there is no point in trying to make any boat point higher than its capabilities. This is called pinching. The boat will slow markedly, but you will still be gaining windward angle, at least until her momentum drains off. In racing, it's sometimes necessary to pinch, but only for short periods under special tactical conditions. In your practice sessions, you might pinch her up to see what it feels like, but practically speaking pinching won't be very effective.

For now, bear in mind this general principle: Windward sailing is a compromise between speed and upwind angle. As you point up, you gain angle, but you lose speed. As you bear away—it's called footing—you will gain speed but lose angle. If you foot off too far, you will essentially be sailing away from your mark. If you pinch, you will be sailing too slow. Some very smart race boat designers and navigators have devoted much thought and many gigabytes of computer power to figuring out the optimum upwind angle and speed for individual boats in all wind conditions. It's a tricky fine line, and even experienced racers aren't able to walk it consistently. But for our practice purposes, your telltales are the best indicators.

If you foot off too far, your outside telltale will droop. If you try to point too high, your inside tale will droop. Assuming you've trimmed the sails sufficiently tight, but not too tight, and your telltales are streaming, you can figure that you're making good an upwind angle of about 50 degrees to the true wind.

HOW MANY TIMES SHOULD YOU TACK?

This, too, is a compromise. Theoretically you could reach (fetch in the parlance) the mark with one tack halfway up the beat. Or you can tack multiple times. There is no difference in distance sailed, all things being equal, which in the real world they seldom are. However, if you sail one long tack, your course will take you far to one side or the other of the straight upwind line, the rhumb line, called "banging the corner" in racing parlance. However, if the wind shifts unfavorably, then you will lose a lot of ground; plus you won't learn as much about the maneuver. On the other hand, boats slow down with each tack, so you don't want to short-tack toward the mark. Instead, let's try to find a happy medium between banging the corner and a lot of short tacks.

Try to stay in the middle. To help you visualize the geometry of your upwind leg, imagine a line running from your mark straight downwind. You're tacking back and forth across that line. Port tack will run to the right of that line, and starboard tack to the left. Unless one tack is heavily favored over the other, try to keep equal the distance run to the left or right of the line. But before you tack back, always get the boat up to full speed. In your early practice sessions, this is more important than the precise length of each tack. The distance gained (or lost) upwind will depend on the quality of the actual tacking maneuver. If you come out of the tack too high, the boat will slow, and you'll lose some of what you gained while sailing on the other "board." If you come out too low, you will be sailing away from the mark. And of course even after a perfectly executed tack, you will need to foot off a few degrees to reattach the wind to the sails before you turn back up to full point.

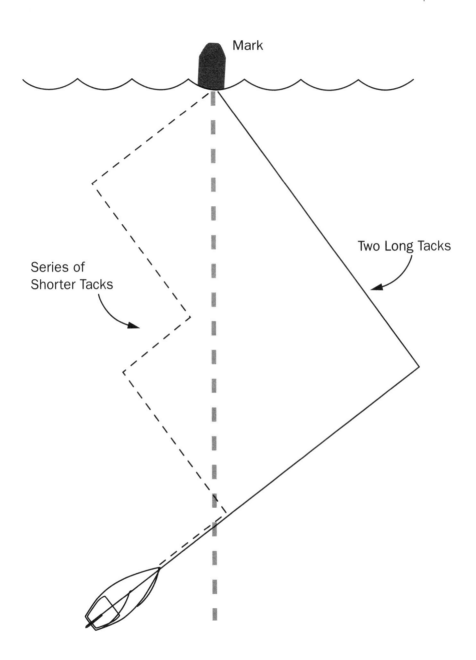

Mark

Two Long Tacks

Series of
Shorter Tacks

Whether you sail two long tacks or a series of shorter tacks, the distance will be the same. However, it's usually more efficient to tack more than once to accommodate wind shifts.

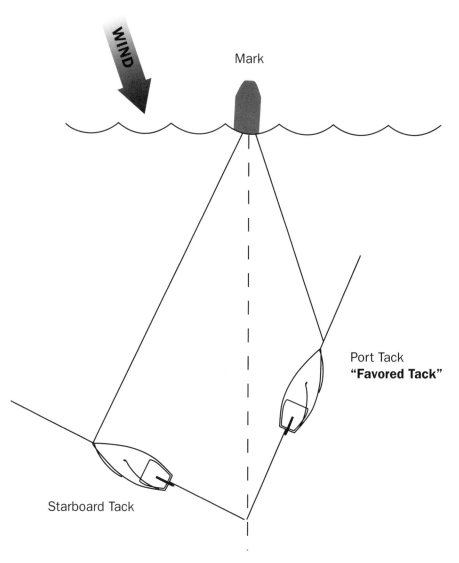

A "header" on starboard tack means that there will be a "lift" on port tack.

WHAT ABOUT WIND SHIFTS?

We get into a rather sophisticated level of sailing by asking you to consider wind shifts in your upwind sailing. You may not be able to accommodate shifts or possibly even notice them in your early practice sessions. However, it will prove useful later to grasp the underlying principle at this point. It can be simply stated: All wind, even steady wind, shifts.

Here is an exemplary situation: You're getting the feel of upwind sailing; you're steering attentively on starboard tack; your jib telltales are streaming nicely. But look—your windward (inside) telltales suddenly droop. You know what that means by now: You're steering too high. So you bear away slightly, and the inside tales stream again. Good. But then the same thing happens. The inside tales droop. Assuming fine, attentive steering and trim, the only other explanation is that the wind is shifting. More precisely, it is shifting toward your bow, that is, from your right to left—to your disadvantage. In the parlance, this is a header, sometimes called a knock. You can still maintain the same angular relationship to the apparent wind by bearing off. The tales will still be streaming, reflecting your growing steering skill, but the new wind direction is now taking you away from your mark. Just how far it's taking you from the mark depends of course on the size (in degrees of the compass) of the wind shift. But since you had to bear away more than once to keep the tales flying, this looks like a progressive left-hand shift that will continue to knock you. (Note that I'm not talking about a radical wind shift, say, from north to west, but a much smaller shift, not more than 20 degrees.)

Before discussing how to recognize the presence and direction of a wind shift, let's run through the opposite situation from a header: a lift. The lift is a wind shift toward your stern. You're still on starboard tack, steering with fresh confidence, tales streaming. But suddenly the leeward (outside) jib telltales droop. As you know by now, that means you are sailing too low. So you come up a few degrees, to reattach the flow to the outside of jib. Now the tales on both sides of the jib are streaming in unison. But it happens again—the outside tales fall limp. So you steer up still farther. The angle between the apparent wind and your centerline has not changed; you're still sailing close-hauled. But the wind is shifting persistently in your favor—the shift is taking you closer to your mark. So you hold that tack, gaining angle.

If you're knocked on one "board," say starboard, then tack over to the other board. A header on starboard tack is a lift on port tack, and vice versa. Sometimes wind shifts are persistent in one direction or the other, either a lift or a header. If it's a persistent header, then you might as well tack over. If it's a persistent lift, then you want to hold that board. Often, however, the wind shifts will oscillate, shifting right (a lift on starboard tack), then left (a header on starboard), and back right again. And often in an oscillating breeze, the shifts will occur at more or less regular intervals. Success in racing will depend on "nailing the shifts," as they say, that is, tacking on the headers, if the shifts are sizable. This tactic keeps the boat pointed closer to the mark most of the time, so you sail a shorter distance and thus arrive there first. When sailing leisurely, you probably won't be tacking on every shift, but when you practice, when you try to sail seriously, it's worth noting at least that the shifts are present.

RECOGNIZING WIND SHIFTS

You can tell visually whether you're lifted or headed by using land references. With the tails streaming, sailing in the groove, sight some point of land beyond your headstay. If the telltales on one side of the jib luff or the other droop, and you compensate by steering up or down, then your bow will change its orientation in relation to that land reference. Is the new point of land upwind of the previous point (closer to your mark) or downwind (farther from your mark)? This will require some practice and experience, implying as it does that you've learned to sail in the groove upwind, but grasp the concept, at least intellectually, at this point.

The other way to recognize a shift is to use your compass. Remember, all the compass knows is what direction, in degrees of a circle, your bow is pointing. Another way to say it is that your compass substitutes more accurately for that "eyeballed" land reference. On hazy days or when you're sailing in open water, land references will be less useful. Let's say for simplicity's sake that you're sailing on starboard tack due north (000 degrees). The inside telltale on the jib stalls. You steer down to compensate. You're turned the bow—the compass will know that. It will now indicate that your bow is now pointing some number of degrees west of north, say 350 degrees.

You've been headed. Conversely, if you've been lifted, the compass will indicate some number of degrees east of north, perhaps 015 degrees.

COMPASSES: THE BARE BONES

The compass disk or card, the thing with all the numbers, doesn't move. It always points at magnetic north. The boat turns, not the compass card. Notice that red line lying across the compass card. That's the "lubber line." The lubber line always points down the centerline of the boat, thus indicating in degrees (from 0 to 360) where your bow is pointing.

The number at which the lubber line is pointing is your heading. That forms one limb of the all-important sailing angle, while the apparent wind direction forms the other limb. And this angle, both limbs together, determines your point of sail. In that sense, your compass is always a useful indicator.

Now let's return to your upwind leg toward your mark, and let's assume that the breeze is steady, no shifts. Remember, we decided (arbitrarily) to round the mark to port—in other words, the mark will be on the left-hand side of the boat as you round it. That means you will have to be on starboard tack when you round. So you've tacked your way up the course, and now, as you sail on port tack, you're almost abeam of the mark. Your next tack—starboard—will take you around. In sailing language, you will "lay" the mark. When do you tack in order to lay it? You could of course sail way beyond the mark on port, tack over, and pass it with hundreds of yards to spare. But that's not exactly what they mean by "laying the mark." Part of this exercise is about figuring out when to tack over on starboard (on the layline) such that you pass the mark "close aboard," say by a boat length. So the essence of the exercise—which will come up time and again in the real world—is to visualize your sailing angle on the next tack. You don't want to be short of the mark, requiring two more tacks; nor do you want to "overstand" the mark by more than two boat lengths, thus sailing extra distance.

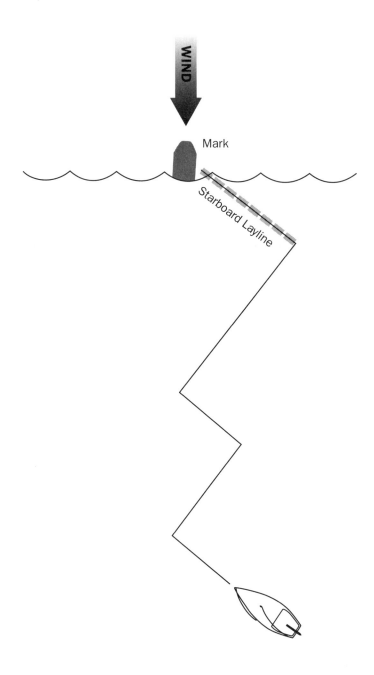

To round a mark to port, you need to approach the mark on starboard tack.

In the real world, there may be variables such as current and wind shifts that will affect your decision as to when to tack onto the layline. It will take practice to "see" the next tack from your present tack, but for now let's state the rule of thumb: Again, it's a matter of visualizing an angle. The centerline of your boat is one limb of the angle, the one indicated by your compass. But you have to visualize the other limb: While on port tack, draw an imaginary line from the mark to the centerline of the boat. The angle between the mark and your centerline is changing—increasing—as you sail along on port. When it reaches 90 degrees, perpendicular to the centerline, then, as they say, you are on the layline. Tack. You will then be able to lay (or "fetch") the mark. If you don't, that's okay; you're just practicing, but try to figure out why you did not pass the mark by a boat length to port. Did you tack too soon or too late? Was your last tack imprecise? Was your steering ragged? Or is something else going on? Current is among the most likely suspects, which we'll consider in chapter 8.

DOWNWIND: THE JIBE

Everything changes when you turn downwind. You may have already experienced the jolt of surprise at the radical shift in conditions, in feel, when you turn abruptly from a beat to a run. The boat slows as the apparent wind plunges, and the sheets go "soft." You're now sailing in a diametrically opposite relationship to the wind—and to the waves. Sailing upwind, you were punching through the waves, but now you're riding them. In all but the flattest of seas, you'll immediately notice the change in motion.

You've rounded your upwind mark to port, which means that you approached it on starboard tack. (Please be sure you understand that fact and why to round an upwind mark to port requires that your layline is a starboard tack. Conversely, had you rounded to starboard, your layline would have been a port tack.) When your stern passes the mark, turn downwind, bear away. To bear away, all you need to do is ease the sails as you turn left. Make the turn slowly, watching the Windex and feeling the apparent shift. Stop the turn when the apparent wind reaches the starboard quarter, a broad reach. You are now sailing on starboard jibe, because the wind is still blowing across the starboard side of the boat, and the boom is out on the port side of the boat. Try edging down a bit farther—in this case that's a left-hand turn of a few degrees—until the Windex points straight aft along the centerline of the boat. You are now sailing dead downwind—"DDW" in the parlance. If you go down any farther, you will be sailing by the lee. You will be nearing the jibe.

A jibe, the opposite of a tack, is a turn in which the stern passes through the eye of the wind. But hang on for a while to get used to the feel of the helm on this downwind point of sail. Give the mainsheet an experimental tug; there won't be much pressure on the sheet because of the decreased apparent wind. Try pulling the jib out on the starboard side, sail wing-and-wing. This, is excellent practice because it requires fine steering to keep the jib flying. (Hint: If you sail just slightly by the lee when sailing wing-and-wing, then the main will deflect the wind directly into the jib, thus helping to keep it full and relatively stable.)

In the decreased apparent, you won't be able to feel the wind as clearly as when beating, so your Windex is your best indicator of wind direction. To repeat, if the arrow moves off the centerline and begins to point toward the mainsail, then you're by the lee. To come up—away from the jibe—turn the bow away from the mainsail. If you turn more than a few degrees upwind, the jib will collapse and fall behind the main. Be patient with yourself when actually trying to run downwind, or when reading about it. A model boat might help you solidify these concepts, all of which relate to that old matter of the angular relationship between the centerline of the boat and the apparent wind direction.

Before getting to the jibe maneuver itself, let's pause to restate the earlier distinction between beating and running with respect to the interaction between wind and sails. Running, the sails eased out as far as possible, there can be no wind circulation on the leeward side of the sails. Therefore, the sail is acting not as an aerodynamic shape, as an airfoil, but simply as an obstruction in the wind's path, something for the wind to push against. Dead down is the slowest of the points of sail, not only because you're sailing away from the wind, thus decreasing the apparent, but because of the absence of circulation around the windward and leeward sides of the mainsail. No lift. Easing the halyard and the outhaul will make the sail fuller, a better downwind shape, but that won't help very much. Dropping the traveler all the way down on the same side as the main will also help a little. You might want to put in some boom vang to tighten the leech. Some sailors would say why sail DDW at all; it's just too slow. However, it's still good practice in helm control in the learning stages.

Jibing

We've been assuming throughout a fine sailing breeze of 14 to 15 knots true. Sailing dead down, the apparent won't be much over 10 knots. It's worth stipulating the apparent velocity because there is huge difference between a light-air jibe and a heavier-air jibe. Now, assuming you're sailing on starboard jibe, boom out on the port side, which way will you turn to jibe? To jibe, you must turn the stern through the eye of the wind—that is, rotate the bow toward the mainsail. In this case (starboard jibe), that will be a left-hand turn.

But turn slowly. Observe your indicators, as always, the Windex especially. Look, too, at the main. The boom might bounce and the sheet sag as the wind begins to go out of the sail. Everything softens; you can feel it. At some point very soon, the breeze will reach the leeward side of the main. The boom will then swing across the cockpit from the port side to starboard. That's the jibe. You've turned the stern through the eye, and the mainsail has flopped to the opposite side. You are now on port jibe. But now we need to look closer at the mechanics, because that swinging boom is a hazard to your health and well-being as well as to the rig. Jibes must be controlled.

In light air, there is nothing to the maneuver. You can jibe "all standing," which is to say you can just turn the boat. The boom will swing gently across the cockpit. In fact, you might have to help it across by grasping the mainsheet and physically shoving the boom over. However, as the apparent wind increases, the jibe becomes decidedly more tricky and dangerous than a tack. During a tack, the mainsail can only flog as your bow crosses the eye of the wind simply because the forward end of the boom is attached to the mast. The aft end of the boom, however, is attached to nothing but the sheet, and a rope will not prevent the boom from slamming across the cockpit. That's why you must control the jibe in any but the lightest air. Take all precautions against the accidental jibe.

As soon as the apparent wind moves aft toward the quarter, you need to start thinking about the threat of an accidental jibe, and all aboard should be aware of the potential threat to their crania. Mind the waves, if any. In a small boat, even relatively small waves can knock the stern around to cause an accidental jibe. Figure out which way you'll need to turn the boat to avoid jibing until you're ready for it. In other words, which way do you need to turn to put the bow toward the wind? It's always the direction away from the boom. Don't get confused about this. (To repeat: In a tiller-steered boat, if you push the tiller toward the mainsail, no matter the point of sail, the boat will always come up toward the wind.) Settle in and, as always, feel the boat. Is she surfing, even slightly, on the waves? You'll know if she surges forward and then falls back with each wave. Is she sailing in a straight line, requiring few helm adjustments, or is she skittish, requiring constant helm attention? Momentarily remove your hand from the helm. What's the boat want to do left to her own devices? Chances are she will want to come up toward the wind and away from the jibe, but not necessarily.

Jibe the boat only when you feel ready and comfortable.

There are various techniques depending on the apparent wind velocity and the size of the boat. On small keelboats such as a J/24 and all centerboard dinghies, the helmsman handles the main sheet. On larger boats, a second person, a dedicated main trimmer, jibes the main. As the helmsman turns the boat by the lee and the pressure comes off the main, the trimmer sheets in fast hand-over-hand to keep the boom under control as it passes over the cockpit. (Everyone aboard should be verbally informed before the jibe that a jibe is imminent. "Watch your heads, we're about to jibe." Then, as the boom begins to move inboard, the helmsman says, "Jibe-ho." Ducking, we might say, is the most crucial part of the jibe.) The trimmer must be careful as he sheets in the as the stern crosses the eye of the wind that the mainsheet does not find its way into its cleat. If it does, then the force of the swinging boom, when brought unintentionally to the sudden stop, could rip out the mainsheet block. That's happened at least once to most of us. Instead, the main trimmer must be ready to let the sheet run through his hands, free of the cleat, maintaining some "braking" tension on the sheet as the boom crosses the centerline. Wear sailing gloves. If the timing between the helmsman and the trimmer is in sync, then you will "jibe soft" by this method. Try never to "jibe hard" to avoid the stress on the gear and anxiety among the crew. Also, a hard jibe can slew the boat, particularly a dinghy, out of control. On a light-air day, practice the maneuver repeatedly.

WHAT ABOUT THE JIB IN A JIBE?

Concentrate on jibing the main. Leave the jib to its own devices. It's not helping you that much anyway. If you were sailing wing-and-wing before the jibe, after the jibe the jib and main will be on the same side of the boat, and the main will blanket the jib. After the jibe, at your leisure, pull the jib to the other side and try to "wing it" again. If you're tired of trying to keep the jib full wing-and-wing, let it hang there behind the main.

Notice, as you practice the maneuver, the huge difference between jibe angles and tacking angles. In a light-air jibe, you barely need to turn the stern as you hand the mainsheet from one side to the other. The tack requires a wide change of heading, usually about 90 degrees. You naturally gain downwind angle in the jibe, but since you're running before extremely diminished apparent wind, you lose speed.

JIBING WHEN THE WIND IS UP

Here you have a decision to make. Don't be overly brave. The best way to experience the jibe in big air, recognizing that that's a relative term, is aboard a boat with an experienced crew. On the other hand, I don't want to be alarmist about the jibe. If you feel ready, go to it. However, when the wind is up, you must not jibe "all standing" without manually controlling the flying boom. The trimmer must haul smartly on the sheet as soon as the sail goes soft when the boat turns, and he must slow the boom as it crosses the cockpit by keeping some tension of the sheet. Don't let it snap to the other side. This is easier said than done.

If the wind is heavy, and you're afraid to jibe, then don't. Practice something else. But what if you're running downwind, the boom out on one side or the other, and you see that in order to get back to your mooring or to clear an obstruction, you have to jibe? No, you never absolutely have to jibe. You always have an escape route to avoid jibing—assuming the absence of rocks or other obstructions nearby. You can always "ware" around to move the boom from one side of the boat to the other without jibing.

WARING

Let's say you're sailing on a run with the main out on the starboard side, that is, on port jibe. Meanwhile, the wind velocity has increased beyond your level of jibing experience or comfort. Yet for some reason, in order to get home, you need to make a course change requiring a jibe. In sailing there is almost always time to think about your alternatives before doing anything. (That said, however, don't sail yourself into danger by letting your concentration lag. Think ahead of the boat.)

Instead of turning downwind, as when jibing, turn upwind—away from the boom. That will be a left-hand turn if you start from port jibe. Trimming in the sails as you turn, take her onto a beam reach, and continue turning right up onto a port-tack beat. Pause there for a moment, square away the trim, and let the boat accelerate. Then tack onto starboard and bear away, while easing the sails, back onto a run. The boom will now be on the other side of the boat from when you started the maneuver. By turning the boat through nearly 360 degrees, you've accomplished the same thing as if you had jibed, but with none of the stress and wear and tear on the gear and the psyches. Waring isn't a particularly elegant maneuver, but it works. (A friend of mine who races a J-105 calls this a Crazy Ivan.)

If/when you decide to jibe in heavy air, consider the apparent wind factor and the waves. Chances are the heavy wind will be gusty. Notice the rhythm of the gusts and lulls. You want to execute the jibe during a lull, when the apparent wind decreases. You can also "soften" the jibe by executing the maneuver while surfing down a wave. The increased boatspeed due to the boost from the wave serves to decrease the apparent wind. But the timing can be tricky. Don't act suddenly. Prepare yourself and your crew by studying and discussing the duration of the gusts and lulls. Try to predict the next gust/lull. Barring local anomalies, the waves will likely be more or less predictable. If the boat is surging forward on the backs of the waves, then the waves need to be considered as well. Feel for the times when, at once, the wind lulls and the boat surfs. That's when you want to jibe. In other words, jibe on top of the wave crest.

Though you don't want to fear the jibe, it deserves real respect in big air. If in doubt, put off the experience until later. That said, when the time comes, the procedure is the same described above—except that it needs to happen faster. The main trimmer needs to haul in the sheet as the boom swings, keeping the line away from the cleat or any other object it might hang up on. And the trimmer needs to "brake" the sheet as the boom swings across the stern. Sometimes it's useful to grasp the multiple parts of the sheet between the boom and the traveler car, braking the boom by that means. But this is not a safe tactic, best left to the experienced sailor.

As you gain experience in heavy air—initially perhaps aboard a boat with experienced sailors—your concept of heavy air will change. What seemed at first overwhelming and a bit scary will begin to feel exhilarating. Still, the heavy-air jibe remains the most dangerous maneuver. Practice the

GOOD EXERCISE

Sail big circles around a fixed object. To do so requires you to exercise all points of sail and the maneuvers in quick order. Don't try to sail too-tight circles, because the boat will stall if, between the maneuvers, you don't allow the wind time enough to attach to the sails. Keep her speed up. Try to keep the mark in the center of your circles. After a few orbits in one direction, turn around and circle the mark in the other direction. Make sure, of course, there are no rocks or other obstructions in proximity to your mark before you circle it. And as always when you're concentrating on your boat and sail handling, don't forget to look for traffic.

For a related exercise, sail figure-eights around two marks in a windward–leeward line.

basic technique of a controlled jibe in light air. Slow everything down in the practice sessions, taking the jibe in incremental steps: Turn the stern slowly; haul on the sheet rapidly. Jibe and jibe again. Take a break; perhaps discuss the technique with your crew. Then jibe some more.

RETURNING TO THE MOORING

If you have a motor, you can turn it on, douse the sails out in open water, and power up to the mooring. Mooring fields can be congested with a lot of expensive marine architecture, which the owners would prefer to remain unscathed, and that's an argument for picking up your mooring under power. And some larger boats are simply not nimble enough to maneuver their way through the crowd. On the other hand, picking up the mooring under sail is much the more elegant way. However, do not try it the first time without practicing the technique out in open water.

The objective is to luff the boat into the wind such that she comes to a stop with her bow over the pickup. The bow person leans outboard, grabs the tall boy to pull the mooring pennant aboard, loops or ties it over the bow cleat, and there you have it. Now the sails—with no sheet tension—are fluttering along the centerline waiting for you to douse them. There two questions to consider: How do you approach the mooring before luffing? And how far will the boat carry her momentum after the sails are luffed? Only practice will answer these questions.

Broadly speaking, how quickly a de-powered sailboat sheds her momentum depends on the weight of the boat and the velocity of the wind. A heavy 40-foot cruising boat will carry on much farther than our light 24-footer in a given wind speed. A flat-bottomed dinghy will stop almost immediately. Any boat will stop more quickly in a heavier wind than in light air; sailboats have a lot of windage. That's the first thing to learn, and you can do so at any time out in open water. All you have do is spin the bow into the wind. You might start from a beat, since in that case the bow is closer to the wind than any other point of sail. What essentially you're doing is intentionally putting the boat in irons, or to say it differently, removing her sailing angle. She stops. This maneuver is valuable enough to include in every practice session whether you ever apply it in a mooring field or not. To get her sailing again, just harden up on the jib and turn the bow. If she's equipped with a genoa overlapping the mast, then turn the bow toward the sail. Otherwise the genoa will backwind and she'll want to tack. So tack her; no big deal. However, the point of the exercise is to make her do what you want, not to respond when she does something you don't. Your Windex remains the best guide. Make the arrow point straight down the centerline. Then practice stuffing her into the wind (after notifying your crew) from a reach, a run, and all points in between. Note the stopping distance, measuring it by eye in boat lengths.

The next step is to practice stopping her at a precise point, essential of course to mooring retrieval. Use something soft and fixed to the bottom—a lobster pot buoy, a lone mooring ball, or a self-made float and anchor—as your target.

For the sake of simplicity, maneuverability, and visibility, you'll probably want to approach your mooring, when the times comes, under main alone. But as a matter of practice, try it in open water with both sails up. Approach your target on a beat. If you meant to round the target, you would wait to tack until the target came abeam, 90 degrees to the centerline. But you don't want to round; you want to stop the boat with her bow over the target. Turn when, or approximately when, the bow is directly downwind of the target and within a couple of boat lengths. This is relatively harder with the genoa up and drawing, because even when unsheeted the flogging sail will tend to pull the bow toward the headsail. But that's why stopping with both sails up is good practice in generally controlling the boat's relationship to the wind. Stopping under control is an important part of sailing. Then take the headsail down and try stopping bow-on to your target under main alone. Our small keelboat will sail admirably well under the main. However, that configuration will likely change the point at which you turn the bow from a beat into the wind. Practice the maneuver repeatedly in various wind and (don't forget) current conditions. You'll probably find that it's simpler in fact than the description suggests. Now let's approach the mooring under the mainsail and continue to assume the presence of our steady 14-knot breeze.

Take a pass along the outer fringes of the mooring field, noting how the boats are lying to the wind and the space between them in order to plan your approach. Moorings are usually set in rows with enough space to sail comfortably between rows. For this reason some people like to sail dead downwind a boat length or two past their mooring, then spin her into wind, letting her coast to a stop within reach of the pickup. However, there is usually room to approach the mooring on a beat, arguably the simpler method, requiring a much smaller turn. (Presumably, you've practiced this in open water.) You don't need speed, so sail a tight beat under the main; just keep her moving so you'll have rudder control. Then when the bow is almost on the mooring, turn her directly into the wind. Remove all sheet tension, so she doesn't keep sailing. She'll stop easily within two boat lengths.

If you come up short, don't worry about it. Harden back up on the mainsheet, put the helm over, repeating the same process as when you dropped the mooring, and sail away. Then come back and do it again, having learned something about the timing. If on the other hand, you're coming in too fast, you can slow the boat by pushing the boom as far out on one side or the other as it will go, and holding it out there in the wind as a very effective brake.

Though wind direction matters most, since you can only stop a sailboat when the wind is forward of the beam, current will need to be considered. If current and wind are both coming from the same direction, then of course the boat will stop more quickly than if the current is on her stern. Current is one of the environmental givens of sailing. Always look for current signs whenever you're sailing, and in this case current will have real effect on your plans. But the point is, don't be surprised by current. Study its signs as you plan your way to your mooring.

Finally, if you have an engine, you might during your initial mooring retrievals turn it on, leave it ticking over in neutral ready to power you out of a jam, should one arise. Before long, you'll be able leave it off or leave it below, and sail up to the mooring as a matter of elegant routine.

7

RISING WIND

THE FAMILIAR, ACTUAL SCENARIO GOES LIKE THIS. Ninety-five boats show up early for the ten thirty start of a large regatta almost anywhere in the Northeast, Southern California, the Gulf of Mexico, and parts of the Northwest. There isn't a breath of wind. We wait. And wait. We banter with old sailing acquaintances as they motor around aimlessly. "It'll fill in," says one dedicated optimist. "Always does." It's hot, and the surface looks like plate glass. Here and there, people go for a swim. Lunchtime comes. And goes. The young and the impatient are getting silly and surly, respectively. "Look, it's filling in," someone says pointing at dark patches off to the southwest. Nope, the dark patches disappear. Not even ripples remain. A few boats have already packed it in, motoring homeward, but most wait. We want to race. It might fill in. But it doesn't, finally the race committee sounds three short horn blasts, signaling cancellation.

Then, before the engine even warms up, the wind fills in from the southwest, our desired direction. "Always happens like that," some sage proclaims. So we stick up the main and the big jib, and beat to windward in light, then moderate breeze. But the wind keeps building, so everyone moves to the high side to flatten the light 30-foot boat. That doesn't do it. We actually reef the main when the apparent gets up into the 20s. And it continues to build until the true wind's honking at 26 knots. We're getting nowhere to windward, beating up the sails for nothing, and we're taking a bit of a beating ourselves. Finally we douse everything to motor home into the teeth of the wind. Sometimes it happens that way, from no wind to more wind than you want in a relatively short while.

I'm talking here about a stiff wind inshore, not a gale in the open ocean. There's no emergency. But the wind is too strong to continue sailing normally. Aggressive steps need to be taken in response. Like what?

In most, but not all, places where people sail recreationally, wind seldom leaps from almost nothing to 25 knots unless a significant weather front is coming on. In that case, you would have been aware of it from the ubiquitous forecasts, or you should have been. Usually the wind pipes up incrementally, and you can take incremental steps. However, when the wind increases enough to make you uncomfortable, then don't hesitate. Shorten sail. Reef her down. You'll be fine.

Ideally, you'll acquire some big-wind experience on someone else's boat with sailors who have seen it all before. But don't count on that. Learn how to reef. I was talking with a young couple who had taken sailing lessons, and they had been enthusiastic, they said, about learning more. But they quit abruptly after being "caught out in a storm," as they put it. They were terrified, they said, rolling their eyes at the memory. I asked about the wind velocity, but they didn't really know, except that it "howled." "Did you reef?" I wondered. Both looked at me blankly as if I'd suddenly changed the subject to snorkeling.

Too bad, I thought, that they had lost something they'd enjoyed to unnecessary fear. All they had to do was reef her down, and their "storm" would have felt like what it probably was—a stiff breeze. Practice reefing on fine days, establish a routine, and then practice doing it faster. Reefing systems today are brilliantly simple, so there is really no excuse.

Not all boats can be reefed. Lightnings, despite their big mains, aren't usually set up to be reefed; J/24 don't usually have reef points. That is to say that their mainsails aren't usually rigged and equipped with reefing gear. But these are race boats; you're supposed to deal with them, if you have to, in 25 knots. Most of the small cruiser/racer keelboats you'll encounter will be equipped with reefing gear for both sails.

REEFING THE HEADSAIL

The majority of small fin-keel cruiser/racers these days are equipped with roller-furling genoas. The mechanism is low-tech, simple, and dependable. The genoa is hoisted in a luff groove on an aluminum extrusion around the headstay. The extrusion is connected to a drum at the foot of headstay. A single control line is wrapped around the drum and led aft to the cockpit. Hauling on the control line causes the drum and the extrusion to rotate, thus wrapping the genoa around the headstay. To re-set a roller-furled sail, all you need to do is uncleat the control line and haul on the sheet. To reef it, ease the sheet and haul on the control line. The sail obediently rolls around the headstay.

When to reef and the specific procedure for doing so will depend on the boat and the opinion of its owner. But as the wind gets up, and the boat begins to feel overpowered—or if the wind strength makes you nervous— try shortening the genoa first. Take the force out of the sail by easing away on the sheet or turning up into the wind, then roll the genoa down to 100 percent such that the foot of the sail fits in the fore triangle. But remember that you'll also have to move the sheet lead forward. As I said earlier, you can't use the same lead for 135 percent when you shorten it down to 100 percent. Don't even try.

Genoa leads, called cars, are usually mounted on tracks bolted to the deck so that the lead can be moved forward as you shorten sail. Some boats are rigged with car-control lines, allowing you to move the lead while the sail is still drawing or "under load," as they say. To move the lead all you need to do is pull or ease the line depending on which way you want to move the car. On other boats, you have to go forward and move the car by hand. If that's the case, you might as well roll the genoa all the way in to keep it from flogging over your head as you take the car forward. (I learned that the hard way many years ago when a flogging clew dislocated a finger.) Set the lead to the 100 percent position, return to the cockpit, then pull the sail back out until it reaches the desired size, and cleat down the control line. If the wind continues to build and you want to further decrease the sail area, you have two choices, depending, as always, on conditions and the particular boat.

One is to roll away the genoa entirely. This works particularly well if you can flatten the main by hauling on the backstay and tightening the halyard. It's easy, then, to spill excess wind from the main by dropping the traveler. In the gusts, you can turn the boat toward the wind to spill force from the main. The other alternative is to reef the main while leaving the genoa at 100 percent. In other words, you've reefed both sails in the interests of balance.

The modern system for reefing the main is called slab or jiffy reefing. The objective is to shorten the main by lowering it. Notice (1) the metal hooks mounted near the gooseneck and (2) the heavily reinforced ring called a cringle about three feet up the main luff. To reef, you ease the halyard until you can slip the cringle over the hook. You've then shortened the main luff. Retighten the halyard. That's step one. Now you need to shorten the leech an equal length. The sailmaker has accommodated this by placing another cringle in the leech at the same height above the foot as that in the luff.

A rope, the reefing line, tied at one end to the boom runs up through the cringle, back down to a block on the other side of the boom, thence forward inside the boom to an exit and a cleat. Hauling on the leech line pulls the leech cringle down to the boom. Cleat down the line, and you've reefed the main. The explanation of the system may be more complicated than the system itself. With practice, one person can reef the main faster than the time it takes to read about it. But there are a couple of caveats worth mentioning.

You won't be able to lower the halyard when the mainsail is full of wind. Spill the wind from the main before you try to reef it. If the wind is forward of the beam, you might be able just to ease away on the sheet until the sail flogs. That of course won't work if the wind is aft of the beam, in which case you'll need to turn the boat up into or near the wind before you reef.

An advantage of a halyard winch mounted on the mast is that it allows one person, in cooperation with the helmsman, to put in a reef. She can lower the halyard, slip the cringle over the tack hook, then haul on the reef line while standing at the base of the mast. If the tail of the halyard is led to the cockpit, you'll be glad to have another crew to ease the halyard so that the person at the mast can hook the luff cringle. As the number of crew necessary for any maneuver increases, the need for communication also increases, another reason why you want to practice reefing in fair weather. Establish a

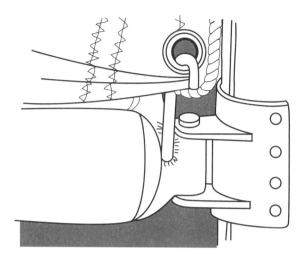

Slab or jiffy reefing system. Both the luff and the leech of the main need to be lowered. The luff cringle is attached to the tack hook; the leech is pulled down by the reefing line.

routine. Reef early; don't wait until you're overpowered and the lee rail is in the water. It's hard to overstress the increased difficulty of doing anything when the wind is blowing hard.

To "shake out" the reef, ease the halyard enough to detach the tack hook. Release the leech line from its cleat, and then tighten the halyard to full hoist. Simple; that's why they call it jiffy reefing.

Most boats have two reef points, called first reef and second reef. This means that there must be two sets of cringles, one atop the other, in the luff and the leech. Therefore, there are two reef lines running forward from the leech in or along the boom, and you don't want to haul on the upper—the second reef line—when you mean to put in the first reef or vice versa. (To distinguish the first-reef leech line from the second-reef line, a friend of mine has colored the tail of the second reef line green on the logic that if conditions require a double reef, he'll likely be seasick.) Many times in the open ocean I've double-reefed the main, but never when sailing inshore. If conditions dictate two reefs, then you'll probably be thinking about seeking shelter in a harbor.

Recognize that reefed sails, main and/or genoa, are not nearly as efficient as full sails, because reefing "misshapes" the sails. This is no good reason not to reef when conditions so require, but don't expect the boat to behave with the same degree of cooperation when she's reefed down. One of the best ways to maintain control under reefed sails is to put the boat on a close reach with the sails a bit undertrimmed. In the gusts—and there will be gusts—poke the bow up a few degrees toward the wind to "feather" the sails. When the gust passes, ease her back down. You don't want to press her up in the gusts so far that the wind finds the lee side of the jib, causing an "auto tack." However, if that should happen, if the jib "backs," then just throw off the jib sheet and let her tack. Sheet in the jib and find the close-reach angle on the new board. Try to prevent the sails from flogging either by sheeting in or turning slightly away from the wind. Prolonged flogging will damage sails and make everyone nervous.

Finally, you need not be frightened of big wind inshore, knowing that you can take steps to accommodate it—if you've practiced the steps in fair weather. Once you've experienced and dealt with wind in the mid 20s, it won't feel so threatening the next time. If you can first experience big wind aboard someone else's boat, better still. Big-wind sailing is not relaxing, but it's usually exhilarating, and it's a great confidence builder to learn that you can successfully deal with a blow.

8

TIDES AND CURRENT SAILING

THERE ARE A LOT OF DIFFERENT KINDS of simultaneous motion intrinsic to sailing. The wind moves. The boat moves, thus altering both the velocity and direction of the apparent wind. And the water moves in the form of currents, altering your course and/or speed over the bottom. Inshore currents, as distinct from permanent ocean currents—the Gulf Stream, for instance—are caused principally by tides.

TIDES

Tides don't exactly roll in and out, nor do they rise and fall. Tides are caused by the combined gravitational pull of the sun and moon, mostly the moon, because it's nearer. It draws up two bulges of water, one extending toward the moon, the other, on the opposite side of Earth, away from the moon. Alternating tides result not from the movement of the water bulges themselves—they remain stationary—but from the movement of Earth rotating beneath them. If you're interested in studying tidal dynamics and their causes, try *Reed's Nautical Almanac, American Practical Navigator,* Vol. I ("Bowditch"), *Tides and the Pull of the Moon* by Francis E. Wylie (Berkley), or conduct your own online research.

For our purposes, let's look at tides from the apparent, local point of view: Tides rise and fall and, with apologies to scientists, they produce back-and-forth horizontal currents. Since sailboats are slow, they spend a lot of time under the influence of a current. Thus, it behooves sailors to know how the current is affecting their course and speed over the bottom.

Some locations experience two high and two low tides a day; others, only one high and one low each day. Because the lunar cycle is longer than the solar cycle, the high and the low tides usually arrive about an hour later every day. When the moon is full and when it's new, the gravitational forces of the sun and moon are aligned and the height of the high and the depth of the low will be greater (called spring tides) than during mid-phases of the moon (neap tides), when the lunar gravitational force acts at right angles to the solar force.

The *range* of the tide refers to the difference in height between high and low tides. The velocity of the tidal current, stated in knots (nautical miles per hour), is called *drift* in nautical language. The drift is usually, but not always, greater in deeper water than in shallow water. The direction of flow is called *set*. Thus, we talk about the current's set in degrees of the compass *toward* which the current is flowing. Note that we talk about wind in the opposite way, the direction from which it blows. Suppose the wind and current are both flowing from the same direction, due east. We would then say that we have an easterly wind and a westerly set.

The tidal range, the current's set and drift, and the times of high and low water for every day are known and in all but a few special cases entirely predictable. That's because astronomers can predict precisely the movements of the moon and sun that cause tidal movement. The tide and its dynamics are interesting per se as well as pertinent to all sailors, but you needn't bother memorizing many facts about tides unless you wish to. All you need to do is look them up in one of many sources. The Weather Channel, local newspapers, almanacs, and numerous Web sites all report the times of high and low tides for different local points, usually harbors. This is useful information, particularly if you intend to enter one of those harbors in a deep-draft boat. More useful for general sailing purposes, however, is information about the tidal current, its set and drift, at a given time of day in your local sailing grounds. To see the current's set and drift graphically illustrated, find a set of current charts.

Tide current charts covering every significant bay, sound, and river in the country are available in nautical publications such as the *Eldridge Tide & Pilot Book* (covering the US East Coast), *Reed's Nautical Almanac*, and on various Web sites, particularly NOAA's. The charts depict the current's set and drift for each hour of the incoming and outgoing tide, its flood and its ebb, respectively. Take a little time at home to study the tide charts for your sailing waters and learn how to read them. This will afford a "big picture" of the current pattern for your sailing area.

Now let's consider how to observe local current behavior from aboard a sailboat, assuming always that you've consulted your sources before you set the sails and that you know whether the tide is ebbing or flowing and when it will change. Will you be sailing in a fair current setting in the same direction as your desired course or a foul current setting against your course? If, for example, your boat is doing 5 knots through the water, and the water is moving against your bow at 2 knots, you will only be making good 3 knots over the bottom. And of course the reverse is true: Riding a 2-knot current at 5 knots of boatspeed means you're making good 7 knots. You can use the fact that the current flows faster in deep water than shallow water to your tactical advantage by ducking into shallow water when the current is foul and riding it in deeper water when it's fair. Remember, however, that you cannot recognize either condition simply by looking at the water. You need to find and use fixed visual reference points.

Anything anchored to the bottom—navigation buoys, lobster pots, exposed rocks, mooring balls, dock pilings, and so forth—will reveal current in the form of a wake flowing around it. (In Maine, for instance, the current often flows fast enough to drive lobster pot buoys underwater.) If you see no wake around anchored objects, chances are the tide is slack, that period of no movement as a flood tide changes to an ebb, or vice versa. Like the current itself, the length of the slack will vary from place to place. But then, you know that, because you've done your homework, consulting tide charts before you stepped aboard the boat.

The shape of the land determines the tide range as well as the velocity of the current—currents accelerate as they try to squeeze into narrowing quarters such as bays and river mouths. The cause of the tide, the gravitational pull of the sun and moon, is universal, but its actual behavior is strictly a local matter. In southeast Florida, for instance, the tide ranges about 3 feet; in eastern Maine, it can range 20 feet.

CURRENT SAILING

When sailing directly up- or downcurrent, your speed of advance over the bottom will be directly affected, but not your course over the bottom. However, your course over the bottom will indeed be affected when sailing across the current. Here's the situation:

You're sailing due south on a comfortable beam reach straight toward a navigation mark (almost any anchored object will do). An ebb tide of 2 knots is setting east against your starboard side. Your compass is dutifully indicating your heading of 180 degrees. You steer carefully for twenty minutes during which your 180 heading does not change. However, you will never reach your mark. While your bow remains pointing south, your boat is being set toward the east, to the right of your mark. You can't feel the boat sliding sideways, and your compass can't help inform you of that fact. It only knows where your bow is pointing, and yours is still pointing south. But you're not making good a southerly course over the bottom. And after a while, you'll see your mark off your starboard bow rather than dead ahead.

Recognizing that your boat isn't always going where her bow is pointing is not only a matter of efficacious sailing—actually getting where you want to go—but also a serious safety matter. Sliding sideways in a current can set you down on the rocks. Yet it can only do that if you're unaware that you are in fact sliding sideways over the bottom. So how can you tell? The boat is moving; so, too, the wind and the body of water on which the boat is sailing. However, the land remains stationary. You can use it to gauge the extent to which the current is pushing you to one side or the other of your desired course; or to put it differently, pushing you away from where it seems you're going.

The best land reference is a range, two vertical objects that line up from your perspective. (In verb form, two objects that align are said to range.) If as you sail along, the objects remain in line, then you can be certain that you're sailing in a straight line. Neither current nor leeway is pushing you off course. The Coast Guard sets range marks as navigation aids to many of the larger harbors, and these are marked on the charts. But you can find your own ranges—that church steeple and the chimney on the red house—everywhere. They offer invaluable visual information, yet they're often ignored.

If the nearer range mark falls out of line to the left of the farther mark, then you have been set to the right. And vice versa. If you want to regain the range—if for instance you're using the range to safely enter a harbor or pass between obstructions—then you *steer toward the nearer mark*.

Whether or not you're using the range for some practical purpose is less important as you practice than to recognize their usefulness as a visual indication of your actual course over the bottom. Ranges are another in the list of visual clues in the environment that will help you see like a sailor and to learn to sail more quickly than if you ignore them. But it's important also to recognize that element of danger when a current sets you off course. What lies downcurrent? Open water or a rock ledge? Before you can answer that question, you need to know which way is downcurrent. You can learn that from the current charts before you go sailing, and while sailing you can glean the actual, local set of the current by observing water flowing around anchored objects and by observing ranges. These observations need to be added to your visual repertoire along with the others we've discussed.

The broader sailing concept to bear in mind is that under certain conditions—primarily when sailing in a crosscurrent or when making leeway sailing to windward—your heading through the water and your all-important course over the bottom will not always be the same.

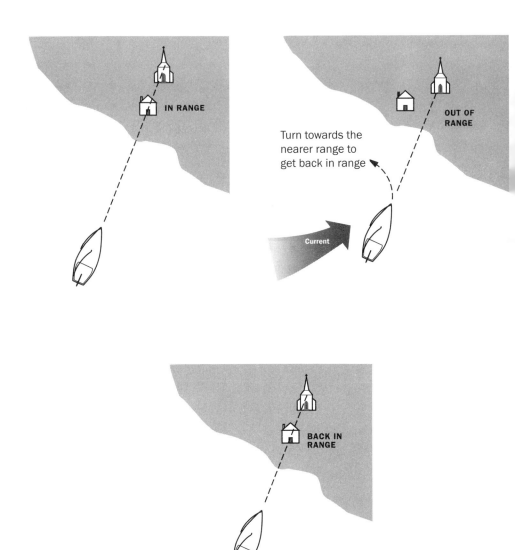

Ranges reveal your true course over the bottom. If current or leeway pushes you "off range," turn toward the nearer mark to return to the range. Ranges are particularly useful when entering harbors.

THE RULE OF TWELFTHS

A long time ago someone divided, for a closer look, the rate of flow in both the ebb and flood into twelve equal parts. The pattern through a single tide goes like this: one-twelfth, two-twelfths, three-twelfths, three-twelfths, two-twelfths, one twelfth. Thus the rule illustrates that the current increases gradually, starting relatively slowly, building to maximum flow in the middle of the tide, then diminishing again as the tide nears slack. However, you can glean this same fact from studying the current charts.

ELECTRONIC AIDS IN CURRENT SAILING

There is really no good reason today not to own a GPS. You can buy an excellent handheld receiver not much larger than your wallet for about $150. Competition among the various manufacturers (Magellan, Garmin, others) is intense, as reflected by decreasing prices. The GPS receiver knows where it is on the face of the Earth from moment to moment. Therefore, it knows how fast you're moving and in what direction you're moving all the time. However, it does not know that you're moving through the water. The GPS reports your course in degrees and your speed in knots over the bottom. Your compass knows what direction your bow is pointing through the water, but it does not know what direction you're moving over the bottom. Likewise, if your boat is equipped with a speedometer, it knows how fast you're moving through the water, but not how fast you're moving over the bottom.

For example: You're sailing on any point of sail at 6 knots according to the speedo. But your trusty GPS receiver reports that you're going 4 knots over the bottom, a speed referred to as velocity made good (VMG). You can then infer by comparing the speed through the water (speedo) with your VMG (GPS) that you're sailing against a 2-knot current. To reverse the example, if your speedo reads 6 knots while the GPS reads 8, then you must be riding a fair current of 2 knots.

Now consider the GPS information about direction over the bottom, or course made good (COG). Say your compass tells you that your bow is pointing at a "heading" of 090 degrees, or due east. Meanwhile, your GPS tells you that your COG is 080 degrees. That means that a current is setting against your starboard side pushing you to the left of your heading. And the longer you stay in that current, the farther you will be set to the left.

The point is this: Unless you're sailing dead upcurrent or dead downcurrent, there will be a disparity between your compass heading and your course over the ground. To put it differently, your boat will actually be going to one side or the other of your heading. This is still another instance of the omnipresence of angles in sailing, in this case between your heading and that all-important direction made good over the bottom, your actual course.

Bigger boats will have a GPS mounted below at the nav station or at the helm drawing power from the boat's battery and receiving information from an antenna mounted topside, often on the stern rail. A handheld GPS, powered by two AA batteries, will not receive any information from the twenty-four orbiting satellites that form the basis of GPS if taken below. Handhelds must be able to "see" the satellites, and so must be used on deck. It is worth repeating that you can glean what you need to know about how rapidly and in what direction the current is setting your boat by eyeballing your course in relation to land references. But by putting numbers to your COG, the GPS is far more precise. What you must not do, with or without a GPS, is forget that in a crosscurrent you will not be going where your bow is pointing, but at some angle in relative to your heading.

9

SAFETY

MOST ACCIDENTS HAPPEN WHEN BOATERS STOP PAYING attention, when they go too fast, when they drink too much, or when they do something really stupid. Thus, most boating accidents are completely avoidable, unlike, say, mountaineering where the climber may do everything with great expertise and still get killed in an avalanche. See the US Sailing Web site, an excellent resource for all aspects of sailing including education and safety. Five to ten times a year, US Sailing sponsors at venues across the country its excellent, inclusive and famous Safety at Sea Seminars (http://ussailing.org/safety). See http://sailnet.com for articles about safety and almost all other aspects of sailing. See also www.nasbla.org for a state-by-state listing of boating safety courses. Or simply Google "boating safety information sources."

You don't need to be an experienced sailor to sail safely; you only need to use your head. That, it might be said, is a politically incorrect statement, seeming to make light of sailing safety. It doesn't. And there is no excuse for not educating yourself about safety, either from printed sources or from one of the ubiquitous classes. I'm assuming throughout this book that, as a new sailor, you will be sailing inshore in gentle conditions, in which case you need not be frightened of the sport—as long as pay attention to what's going on outside as well as aboard your boat, think ahead, and use your common sense. However, there are certain dangers specific to sailing.

See that aluminum spar overhead? The boom? It can kill you. On a big boat, you can stand up in the cockpit under the boom or behind it, but as soon as you leave the cockpit and stand at the side rails, the boom becomes a potential threat. In small boats, it is always a looming threat. Think about where the boom is situated at all times, but especially when the wind goes aft of the beam and the boom is eased outside the lifelines. On a run, when an accidental jibe is possible, think of the boom as a lethal instrument. All you need to do is be ready to duck, but you won't be if you're distracted or otherwise unaware of the boom's position in relation to the wind angle.

To say you should wear a personal flotation device (PFD) even in bright daylight on a light-wind day would be to preach what most of us don't practice. (Offshore, I wouldn't step out of the companionway without flotation and/or a safety harness.) But I would certainly draw an embarrassed last breath if I fell off the boat and drowned in 2 knots of wind within sight of shore. It can happen and has; you can drown in any water, no previous experience necessary. Further, PFDs have grown smaller and far more comfortable than the old lifejackets. If you feel like donning a PFD when no one else aboard is wearing theirs, by all means don't let perceived "social pressure" prevent you from doing so. Maybe the day will come when the Coast Guard requires all boaters to wear flotation—you are presently required to carry enough type-one life jackets for everyone aboard—but for now this remains a personal decision. Children should wear PFDs at all times.

But whether you're wearing flotation or not, the first rule of safe sailing is: Stay on the boat. Almost everyone has heard the old maxim, "One hand for the ship, one hand for you." Obey it. Most sailboats bigger than dinghies come equipped with lifelines surrounding the decks. And unlike powerboats, there are many natural handholds on sailboats—shrouds, lifelines, the mast. Use them, even when it doesn't seem necessary. Stay low as you move around the deck, and never run on a deck. If you're learning on a dinghy, a 420, say, or a Laser, you will at some point capsize, so wearing a PFD in all but the lightest conditions is essential. These boats will not sink when they capsize; they'll simply float on their beam ends, the sails lying flat in the water. Generally, to right a dinghy you first release the mainsheet entirely, stand on the centerboard, and pull the rail toward you. But this is just a generalization. All sailing courses using dinghies will include the techniques for righting the boat after a capsize, and there is plenty of literature on the subject. Do not ignore this aspect of small-boat sailing, and remember that different boats are righted with varying techniques.

A major difference between powerboats and sailboats is speed. There is seldom any need to move fast on a sailboat, but even if the need should arise, there is always time to move from handhold to handhold. The only times I've ever been injured on a sailboat were when I grew excited and moved hastily without thinking through the move. I don't do that anymore, no matter what.

MAN OVERBOARD

This is not the appropriate space to explain the various methods of man overboard (MOB) retrieval, but, again, voluminous information is available on the Internet and in books (see *The Annapolis Book of Seamanship* by John Rousmaniere for instance). However, as a matter of practicality and of practice, you'd do well on a fine day to throw overboard a flotation cushion or something and then retrieve it under sail. You'll notice that it's easier said than done. Take that fact seriously, and obey rule number one: Stay on the boat. The man overboard risk has become an issue among those who sail as a couple in which one member is more experienced than the other. What if the experienced sailor goes over the side, leaving the other alone with no clear understanding of how to pick up the MOB, not necessarily a man? This, a serious question, has induced the less experienced members to go take sailing lessons, all of which touch upon MOB retrieval methods. The Cruising Club of America has developed the daylong Suddenly Alone seminars to address this issue. See www.cruisingclub.org. Alternatively, couples should read all the literature about MOB situations and practice the techniques.

HAND INJURIES

One among many intrinsic aspects of sailing that have no dry-land precedent is the necessity to handle lines under load. A lot of force (weight) is lodged in the sheets and other control lines, especially when the wind pipes up. When a line under load accidentally detaches from a cleat or winch and zings off on its own, your first instinct will be to grab it. *Don't.* Let it go until the load comes off. Wear sailing gloves. Jib sheets wound on winches are perhaps the most likely sources of hand injuries. Watch how experienced sailors handle loaded lines on winches. This is strictly a mechanical action, but it won't come naturally. It must be learned through practice. You can more or less gauge sailors' experience by watching the way they handle lines under load. New sailors frequently take too few turns of the sheet around the winch. Take multiple turns, at least three (always clockwise), around the winch, the better to control the load. To detach a line from the winch—as when tacking—pull straight up on the tail of the line, and keep your fingers safely above the winch. Practice line-handling techniques on light-air days. Also, get in the habit of removing the handles from the winches after grinding the winch. Falling on an active winch handle can cause serious injury.

HITTING THINGS

Namely, other boats and the bottom. Collisions are easily avoidable by applying common sense, constant vigilance, and knowledge of the right-of-way rules. To avoid running aground, however, requires at least a rudimentary knowledge of navigation. (Technically, conning a boat within sight of land is called piloting; navigation happens in the open ocean. But in common usage, the distinction has faded away.) You will need to learn, at the very least, how to read a nav chart.

Buy a NOAA chart of your local water in the biggest scale possible (big scale = small area). That will give you the best detail. Study the chart carefully, and keep it aboard or bring it to the boat with your other gear. Then, once you're out on the water, compare the charted features with actuality. Learn how to measure distance on the chart and to notice how distance, say one nautical mile, appears to your eye in the real world.

You'll notice numerous symbols, a kind of shorthand code, unique to nautical charts. To crack the code, buy NOAA Chart No. 1, not really a chart but a booklet containing keys to all chart symbols. Spend some time comparing the actual chart with Chart No. 1. Pay particular attention to buoy designations. Collectively called aids to navigation, buoys come in different shapes, colors, and purposes. All obstructions will be charted, though not necessarily buoyed, and the chart symbols for obstructions will differ according to their nature (wrecks, reefs, submerged cables, etc.) It seems that every small harbor has a particularly treacherous spot, usually a reef or rock ledge, on which boaters regularly come to grief. Local sailors are good sources of "local knowledge," and by all means ask questions, but don't take anything for granted. The paper chart is the final authority.

Naturally, I'd suggest you learn the techniques of coastal piloting—from either books or classroom courses—but you don't absolutely have to while learning to sail. However, what you must never do is set sail anywhere without chart knowledge of what lies below the surface.

GPS is certainly the most significant contribution to navigation since the chronometer. If you want one, fine. I suggest, however, that you learn to read a chart and do your basic piloting by eye and by hand at the early learning stages.

IN CONCLUSION

HERE ARE A FEW SUCCINCT SUGGESTIONS (AND repetitions):

Relax. Sailing isn't all that difficult or mysterious. Try to eliminate performance anxiety. You're bound to make mistakes at first—everyone does—without serious repercussions. Don't be overly critical of yourself or grow frustrated by your mistakes. Remember that even the saltiest sailor with thousands of miles in the log was once a rank beginner grappling with the same concepts and unfamiliar techniques and making the same mistakes as you. What seems mysterious and confusing this season will become second nature by late the next season.

Shoreside study will accelerate the learning process. You can learn the language of sailing in your living room. Likewise, you can learn the basic knots (start with three, the bowline, clove hitch, and reef knot) while watching television. Also, carefully study the point-of-sail diagram in this and other books and magazines. When ashore, you can also study the chart of your local sailing grounds.

However, sailing is not an intuitive sport, at least for most people. Only experience, only time in the boat(s), will avail the learning process. Get on the water as soon and as often as possible on any boat available to you. You'll learn more quickly in a small, responsive boat than in a big boat. Remember always to feel the boat, attune yourself to her motion, acceleration and deceleration and try to figure out what it's telling you. But no matter what boat you sail in the early stages, don't be a "passenger" along for the ride even if you aren't actually participating in the sailing. Notice everything. Watch the crew's actions and timing during tacks and jibes. Don't be hesitant to reveal your ignorance. Ask questions of experienced sailors. Not only will questions and answers speed your learning process, they will demonstrate your avidness and willingness to learn.

Focus first and always on the wind. Think about the wind in terms of the angles it forms in relation to the centerline of the boat. Remember that boats sail to the apparent, not the true, wind. The apparent wind will always seem stronger when you're sailing into it and lighter when sailing "away" from it. Except when you're running dead downwind, the apparent wind angle will always be forward of the true wind. Practice searching for wind signals in both the natural and the manmade environment, including other sailboats. Watch the Windex—it will always point to the apparent wind. Remember also that sailing is a sensual sport. Feel the wind on your face, your arms, and so on.

Remember to look up. It's a sailboat. Everything begins with and proceeds from wind in the sails. Practice visualizing the flow of wind in and around the sails as though the wind were a visible fluid. When you tighten or loosen a sail control, try to focus not on the mechanical action, but on the reason why you're doing so. Look up to see the effect of your adjustment on the sails and on boatspeed. This is another reason why small-boat sailing will be more efficacious than big-boat sailing. Adjustments, even small ones, will have immediate sensual results; in a 40-footer, on the other hand, they will be far harder to notice, in which case the speedo will be useful.

Try right at the start to see and understand the big picture. When you're sailing in a straight line, practice visualizing what will need to be done with the sails and the helm if, say, you were to turn 90 degrees to the right. Will you have to tack (or jibe) or will you need only to ease (or tighten) the sails? Another way to put the question is to ask yourself: Where will the apparent wind be coming from in relation to the centerline of the boat if I make a big (or a small) turn? Unless you happen to be innately talented (and some sailors are), you will find this confusing at first. But the quicker you learn to see the big picture, as opposed to the individual, mechanical actions, the quicker you will climb the learning curve.

You don't have to take a sailing course to learn to sail, but formal training has certain obvious advantages. Most instructors have spent time thinking not only about sailing, but also about how to teach it, two different things. You won't be an accomplished sailor upon completion of the average sailing course, but you'll have a firm foundation in the basics. You'll know how to tack and jibe, at least in rough terms. If you find the basic course useful and pleasing, if you like the instructor's mode and methods, consider taking a more advanced course.

There are many different kinds of sailing—leisurely daysailing, weekend or longer cruising, racing—but try at first to be open to all sailing experiences as you learn the basics before you decide what kind of sailing you wish to pursue. Chances are, you'll want to pursue more than one.

Sail at every opportunity with more experienced sailors. Remember that owning a boat, particularly when money is an object, is a demanding responsibility. Accepting that responsibility implies a love for and commitment to the sport. Thus, in most cases, owners want to spread their enthusiasm to beginners. If you evince your own enthusiasm, you will be welcomed aboard, and pretty soon you'll be asked, "Do you want to take the helm?" Sailing with experienced people is also an excellent way to experience heavier wind in safety. If you've recently bought your first boat, invite experienced people to go sailing with you.

Don't hesitate to fiddle with the sail trim. "When in doubt, let them out." That is, ease the sails until their luffs flutter, then trim them in just enough to stop the flutter. Make small adjustments one at a time, and notice the boat's behavior in response to each. Does she slow down or accelerate? Does she heel or straighten? Try to answer the questions through observation and then try to figure out why she so responds.

Practice stopping the boat either by casting off the sheets or by sticking the bow into the wind. Remember, you can always stop the boat by either method.

When practicing the maneuvers, tacking or jibing, do so repeatedly, leaving time between each for the boat to get back up to speed. (You will lose more speed in a tack than in a jibe. Why?) Take a break after a series of drills and discuss what you've learned with your mates. Then resume the drills. Shift positions; steer for while, then trim for a while.

Different boats will behave differently in tacks and jibes, depending mainly on their size. Bigger boats will take longer to slow down and to accelerate than smaller boats, simply because heavier objects carry more momentum than light ones. This in turn will affect how you handle the helm particularly in the tacks. You can let big boats carry their own momentum through the tacks, which means that you can tack more slowly. The opposite is true in small boats, especially dinghies.

When steering, it's useful to find a stationary point to "aim" at. However, do not focus on that point alone. You'll learn very little by that means. Hold the helm, tiller or wheel, loosely; let it "talk" to you. The feel of sailboat's helm is one of its most articulate means of communication. Practice letting your eyes rove around the various indicators—the Windex, the telltales, the aiming point, the speedo, if any, and the feel of the wind on your face and arms—but depend on them in combination, not one to the exclusion of the others. Make small helm adjustments when you're sailing in a straight line, while bearing in mind that if the wind angle or velocity changes, then a change in trim is necessary.

When tacking, a boat makes a far larger turn than when jibing. Before a tack, get in the habit of finding an aiming point lying about 90 degrees to windward—that's roughly where the bow should be pointing on the other tack. You can come up closer to the wind, after the tack is complete and the boat has regained lost speed, by turning the helm and trimming (tightening) the sails.

Tacking is easier and safer than jibing, because in a jibe, the boom swings freely across the cockpit. Practice jibing in light air. Only a relatively small turn is required to jibe, and sometimes in light air especially you'll need to help the boom across by gripping the sheet between the traveler and the boom and shoving the boom over. In heavier air, this is not a safe practice. In that case, smartly trim in the mainsheet as the boom comes across, and then keep some manual tension on the sheet to slow the boom as the stern passes through the eye of the wind. Jibing safely will require more practice than tacking. But again this is only a mechanical move, and once you have it down, you can begin to consider jibing in bigger air.

Remember, you almost never absolutely have to jibe if the maneuver makes you nervous—say, if the wind pipes up. You can always ware around. Finally, never allow an accidental jibe. A good way to avoid an accidental jibe is to figure out—as soon as you ease the boom outside the lifelines—which way you'll need to turn the bow to avoid the jibe. In other words, which way will you need to turn to "come up" toward the wind? (In a tiller-steered boat, if you put the tiller toward the mainsail, you will always come up, and vice versa.)

Communicate with the other people aboard. If you mean to tack, inform your crew. "Ready to tack?" or "Ready about?" Give them time to prepare and wait for their response. "Ready here." The same of course applies to the jibe, or perhaps more so, because of that swinging boom. You might also remind your mates when on port tack, since on port you relinquish your right-of-way.

Perhaps the most important rule of seamanship is: Keep constant vigilance. Look outboard for other boats or obstructions to safe navigation. While learning, you will tend naturally to focus on your sails and other inboard matters. Remind yourself and your crew to look around. "Do you see that tugboat?" "Do you see the starboard tacker?" "We're approaching shallow water." The foot of some genoas reaches all the way back to the forward edge of the cockpit. This makes it difficult to see boats or objects to leeward. In that case, someone must look around the headsail. Remember also that when sailing to windward, all boats will slide sideways, or make leeway, to some extent. Due to either leeway, current, or both, the boat will not always actually be going in the direction the bow is pointing. This is another instance when seeing the big picture is both safe and seamanly.

And finally, fair winds to you.

INDEX